# The 16-28 Solution

# The 16-28 Solution- Unleash the Passions of Your Youth:
# Five Big Lessons to ReIgnite Your Career

*Douglas Campbell III*

www.TheSuccessCoach.com

Success Coach Publishing

7 Alpine Lane

Darien CT 06820

doug@thesuccesscoach.com

16-28: Unleash the Passions of Your Youth…

# CONTENTS

16-28: Unleash the Passions of Your Youth...

# Dedication

To my youthful children, Colin and Caroline, who have always inspired and surprised Gwynne and me with their choices and decisions along the way. They have journeyed far, leveraged their creativity, and found great success along the way in Ohio, Massachusetts, Pennsylvania, California, Italy, and Australia. Most of all, they have been true to their 16 - 28 passions throughout their lives.

# Acknowledgements

Brandon Toporov was very helpful in developing and capturing the key ideas in this book. Dierdre Silverstein efficiently helped focus and restructure some of the presentations in the book. N. M. Scuri provided much needed editorial advice and feedback. Charlie Hart of Kensington Books was always been helpful and encouraging, and Patti Manzone executed another strong and captivating cover.

There are numerous other supporters along the way who encouraged and challenged. I also would like to acknowledge my High Talent Creative (http://www.thesuccesscoach.com/hightalentcreatives.asp) attendees and the many talented entrepreneurs who have showcased their business and creative stories in an open and sharing manner. Finally, innumerable thanks to the many great people I have met and connected with on the journey. It has been an incredible ride for which I am continually grateful.

*"If what you're doing is not your passion, you have nothing to lose…. Remembering you are going to die is the best way I know to avoid the trap of thinking you have something to lose. You are already naked. There is no reason not to follow your heart."* — Steve Jobs

*"If you look at an obstacle as a containing fence, it becomes your excuse for failure. If you look at it as a hurdle, each one strengthens you for the next."* — Ben Carson

16-28: Unleash the Passions of Your Youth…

# Why I Wrote this Book

Many clients have been fun and inspiring to work with. They have allowed me to get to know them in depth through assessments, questionnaires and lengthy discussions. This has revealed and helped define their 16 - 28 history and passions. In many cases, our work has unearthed some of those lost passions and provided a framework for making key career and life choices. Reinventing your business or your career should explore your early adulthood and its successes. It was a time to "grow new branches on your tree" and broaden your set of experiences. During this 16 - 28 timeframe, there were clubs and internships, part-time jobs, cross country and foreign travel, and early adulthood mentors, jobs and meetings. Each introduced you to new people, new ideas and new opportunities. Which were most important to you? Why?

At times, clients and business partners needed an "unpeel the onion" strategy to reveal true early adulthood passions. One client didn't value anything strongly until I asked the fourth question which revealed an *emotional* answer. He was a tour guide at a school and liked "being part of the community" of classmates, administrators, parents and potential visiting students. In his current work he was at home and isolated representing two small publications selling advertising — a far cry from 25 years at a major business publication. He was frustrated, but immediately began to focus on schools and organizations where there was a strong sense of community. The result was a new energy in a school where he thrived.

As an Executive Coach, I help clients grow and reach new levels of success in their businesses and careers. Over many years of working with my consulting clients, I saw a clear pattern

16-28: Unleash the Passions of Your Youth...

emerging in a number of my most successful interactions. The pattern I noticed suggested that a close, conscious evaluation and study of one's past is a reliable way to chart a truly successful future.

I can't pretend to be the first person to notice this pattern … but I do believe that I'm the first to tie career breakthroughs to the guided review of a specific twelve-year span at the dawn of adulthood, the years between 16 and 28. The five cases I present in the pages follow feature clients who learned something important about their own way forward in the later decades of their professional life. They did that by studying the key decisions and lessons that lay within those 12 years of what I've come to call "Emerging Adulthood."

I've changed all the names and many of the details out of respect for the privacy of the clients and those in their circles. But the core lesson in each case study remains unchanged. On the theory that many other solutions may lie within the experiences of those important early years, I've entitled this book *The 16-28 Solution-Unleash the Passions of Your Youth: Five Big Lessons to ReIgnite Your Career.*

The guiding principle here is that each of us has something important to learn in later life — and perhaps more to learn than we may have imagined — from casting our minds back to those critical experiences of Emerging Adulthood. This was the critical period when we began to settle on who we were going to be as adults.

I've added some insights about my own 16 - 28 years in an Appendix. I hope you will feel free to share your own insights and conclusions on your own 16 - 28 years by emailing me at doug@thesuccesscoach.com.

16-28: Unleash the Passions of Your Youth…

## The 16 - 28 Solution

Before we look at the cases, I want to present the key ideas you'll see throughout this book.

# Compass

We each have a compass like that, a compass that tells each of us what feels right and what feels wrong on an individual level about our own career choices.

The thing about internal compasses is that they only work for one person. Others working at that same company over a similar or the same time span could have chosen, and indeed did choose, to stay on. For others, though, the alarm bells went off, and once they did, they made a change.

That compass was and is connected to a period from his late adolescence and early adulthood that I call the 16 - 28 window.

Events, emotions, experiences, and aptitudes from that critical formative period in our lives are, I believe, what cause the alarm bells to go off for us whenever our careers reach important points of transition ... and they are also what allow us to heed these alarm bells in a way that can eventually allow us to identify our own right next step.

### Finding the Compass Point

*"He who has a why to live for can bear almost any how."*
— *Friedrich Nietzsche*

When I was a teenager, I injured my back quite badly, fracturing a vertebrae. This injury was one of the major turning points in my life. The setback initially seemed like a misfortune that could not possibly lead to anything positive in life. How wrong I was about that! The injury to my back eventually led me to find the compass point by which I would navigate much of my adult life.

Neither the injury's seriousness, nor the length of time I would have to spend recovering from it, were immediately obvious. It eventually became clear to me and to my family, though, that this physical setback was going to be a major challenge that would take a long time to address. We went to dozens of doctors, most of whom played by the rule that, if you didn't know about something or don't have a solution, the last thing in the world you would ever do was admit that to a patient. Most of what they recommended didn't work. In the end, we wasted a lot of time and money on a lot of experts who weren't really experts. The doctors we finally found who did know what they were talking about ended up recommending a course of therapy that took me out of commission for a while. My days as a school athlete were largely over, which hurt in more ways than one, and I spent the better part of two summers on my back. That gave me a lot of time to think.

As I lay there, I learned three important lessons.

First, I learned how to fight through pain and tough times. I learned the importance of a positive mental attitude, which is something I studied and read about as much as I could over those two summers.

Second, I learned how important it was to be able to empathize with others who had encountered major obstacles in their lives — obstacles that nobody else could possibly understand without

16-28: Unleash the Passions of Your Youth…

4

experiencing them directly. That's the kind of obstacle I had run into, but I knew I couldn't possibly be the only one. Suddenly, I had a lot more compassion for people undergoing difficulty than I had had before my back injury. I moved from feeling self-pity about my own situation to acknowledging that there were many, many people who had far less in their lives than I did, but who had somehow found a way to be grateful.

Third, I learned that dealing constructively with limitations is a big part of any well-lived life. Even though each of us faces limitations that are unique to us as individuals, it's also true that we can experience growth when we learn to adapt to those limitations. I began to get excited about the possibility of using my life and my experiences to help other people who were facing big obstacles.

I realize it sounds insane when I say it now — and it certainly would have sounded insane to me then — but I learned lessons from that back injury that eventually made it look like one of the best things that ever happened to me.

Here's what happened. A few years after the summers I spent on my back, once I had healed enough and I could compete on a limited basis in some sports, I realized I could lead a comparatively active life. I found myself in college, taking a class with a teacher I really respected, whom I will call Dr. Behling. He was an important early mentor for me.

Dr. Behling mentioned an opportunity to do some tutoring in Chicago with young kids — five and six years old — whose families were part of a local Mohawk Indian tribe. Today, we would call the kids "at risk" because of the prevalence of alcoholism and other kinds of dysfunction in some of these families, and because of the lack of educational facilities and

16-28: Unleash the Passions of Your Youth…

resources available to the kids where they lived, on a reservation near downtown Chicago.

Without the tutoring help, Professor Behling explained, these kids might not be able to develop at grade level in their early reading skills … but with this kind of help, they'd be in a better position to overcome some of the built-in obstacles in their lives.

When Dr. Behling said that, something inside of me clicked. I knew little to nothing about teaching five-year olds, but I volunteered to tutor those kids from the Mohawk tribe.

## True North

*"Because God is never cruel, there is a reason for all things. We must know the pain of loss; because if we never knew it, we would have no compassion for others, and we would become monsters of self-regard, creatures of unalloyed self-interest. The terrible pain of loss teaches humility to our prideful kind, has the power to soften uncaring hearts, to make a better person of a good one."*
— *Dean Koontz*

I believe — and this is the premise of everything that follows in this book — that identifying your own True North involves looking closely at the skills, aptitudes, and interests that got you past the greatest challenges of your late adolescence and early adulthood. Those skills, aptitudes, and interests are worth understanding and examining closely, because they are what allowed you to find purpose in those early challenges you faced.

The greatest challenge of my own late adolescence and early adulthood was my back injury. But without it, I never would

16-28: Unleash the Passions of Your Youth…

have developed the compassion necessary to get enthusiastic about the possibility of tutoring those kids.

That teaching encounter with the kids in the Mohawk tribe was a life-changing experience. It left me inspired, excited, and focused in a way that was utterly new and exciting. It left me feeling as though all my earlier experiences in life, including but not limited to my back problems, had added up to something unique and important. A psychologist might tell you that, by volunteering to teach those kids, I had just established an element of my identity as a young adult. Of course that would be correct. Another way to describe what had happened to me, though, was that I had found my compass point and then begun moving purposefully toward the True North of my life, the direction that made the most sense for me both personally and professionally.

For me, True North involves giving back through teaching, leading, supporting and helping people over limitations and obstacles to find their best path forward in life. My True North is rooted in the concept of empathy, in understanding and serving others who have encountered limitations large, small, or somewhere in between in the course of their lives.

I couldn't even begin to tell you how many of my most important life experiences align with this True North direction of mine, but here's a brief sampling. The most rewarding elements of my career, including my early work in education, this book, and my coaching practice, have all been built around this concept of supporting people as they encounter roadblocks, and helping them to find the best path over, under, around, or through those roadblocks, whatever form they might take. And of course, all of the charitable work I've done over the years, including one-on-one work with the poor throughout the

16-28: Unleash the Passions of Your Youth...

Americas, Alzheimer's patients, leukemia patients, and group work through various health-related charities, has pointed me in the same True North direction.

Notice that this is my True North, not anyone else's. This North on the compass of my life is unique to me and connected to my specific experiences. It's a life direction that I have learned to identify with relative ease every time I am faced with a major life decision. Decision making tends to be easier or at least more rewarding in the long run, when you know what does and doesn't constitute True North in your own life.

Here are three points that should be part of any meaningful search for your own True North.

First, the True North does not change dramatically over time. It is a thread that runs identifiably through the most rewarding, motivating, and purposeful positive experiences of your life.

Second, it always correlates directly with your own ability to do good work and make meaningful contributions.

Third, it is usually traceable to important choices and experiences that take place between your sixteenth and your twenty-eighth year.

## The Career Options Wheel

*"To map out a course of action and follow it to an end requires some of the same courage that a soldier needs. Peace has its victories, but it takes brave men and women to win them." — Ralph Waldo Emerson*

At various points in my discussions with clients, I ask them to arrange all of what they currently considered their "A list opportunities" into a visual brainstorming display that I call a

16-28: Unleash the Passions of Your Youth…

8

Career Options Wheel. Basically, this is a diagram of your best current options. There's a central circle representing you, the person who's trying to figure out what comes next in his or her professional life and that circle in the middle is surrounded by a group of outer circles, each of which are connected back to the circle in the middle by a line. The larger the outer circle is, the more attractive the potential opportunity is to the person whose name appears in the middle.

These maps are not binding in any way; they just give you a snapshot image of where you think you are and what you are now looking at pursuing with the greatest level of enthusiasm. You can create a Career Choices Wheel at any stage of the process we're talking about, but in my experience they tend to be more meaningful and more useful once you have created the 16 - 28 Narrative that gets you closer to understanding what True North is for you as a person.

It's often quite interesting to compare early Career Options Wheels with later ones. During the first few weeks of my discussions with clients, their Career Options Wheels become more refined and realistic. You'll see this in the cases.

## The Right Move

*"None are so old as those who have outlived enthusiasm."*— *Henry David Thoreau*

Over the course of a number of weeks, my clients and I are able to use our sessions together to leverage the experiences of late adolescence and young adulthood in a powerful way.

By chronicling those experiences, examining them closely, and identifying the lessons that they show us how a client responded to an important early challenge in his life, we are able to draw

16-28: Unleash the Passions of Your Youth...

some conclusions. Specifically, we are able to identify what remains central in their continually revised understanding of themselves and their mission in the workplace. Just as important, we are able to get some clarity about what motivates them, what makes them feel passionate, engaged, and committed — and what doesn't.

Over and over again, I have found, in working with my clients, that the 16 - 28 coaching process that I am describing here is one of the most reliable tools for determining what someone is likely to become excited about. Experience — not just my own — has also shown that focusing someone's attentions on a career path for which he or she has little or no personal enthusiasm is a losing gambit, no matter how successful that career path may appear to someone else. Experience has also shown that, once someone has connected with a career option that truly resonates with him or her, it can deliver extraordinary rewards, no matter how unlikely or uninspiring that option may seem to someone else.

## Many Options

In a very real sense, my clients and I discuss not just career management strategy, but life management strategies.

To do that, we look closely at just about everything of significance that had come before in their life — not just over the past ten or fifteen years, but also in the years of adolescence and young adulthood. Once we identify the key themes, we could see how they might help us to revise a list of five or six options down to a more manageable list of two or three.

In evaluating my clients' own assessments of their lives and careers, as well as the input of others who had lived with, worked with, and shown an eagerness to help them find the right move forward, I noticed that there were a number of themes came up again and again in our discussions. These are:

* Ethics

* Community

* Values

* Leadership

* Family

## The Honest Broker

*A "coach" is a person who gives training, advice, or guidance on a particular subject. Someone who emerges as a good coach for you about career and business matters will be objective, patient, flexible, pragmatic, and strategically minded. A good executive coach will also be ready to push you a little when circumstances warrant, but will usually adopt a casual, non-authoritarian tone in doing so. Your coach should be someone you enjoy talking to.*

That word "coach," seemingly familiar and easy to understand, actually requires a little explanation. In my experience, most

16-28: Unleash the Passions of Your Youth...

people are used to thinking of a coach as someone who changes everything, someone who supplies a whole new wave of techniques, or a critical new infusion of previously unimagined tactics, or maybe even a whole new set of goals that totally transform the individual or team being coached. Most people who talk about coaches are inclined to think of a coach as someone who engineers some kind of total makeover that's applied from the outside and leaves the person being coached totally transformed.

This is not the kind of coaching I'm talking about. What I'm talking about is a series of meetings with someone who has the distance and objectivity, the time, the ability to listen proactively to serve as an effective sounding board, ask relevant questions, and help people connect the dots themselves, so they use their own resources and experiences and insights to make the very best decision ... the personal decision that must always come first when you face a career crossroads. I consider this person an Honest Broker.

There is power in honesty, and great power in honesty that makes it more likely for you to make the right choices in life. It's very likely that people who love and care for you will ask you what you plan to do next, and it's even possible that they may encourage you to pursue one employment lead or another. As valuable as their support, their guidance, and their networking help is, it is nevertheless extremely important that you make this decision for yourself, instead of allowing someone else's expectations to take over the process.

How long should you be willing to answer "I'm still working on that?" At least until you have:

* Finished reading this book.

16-28: Unleash the Passions of Your Youth…

* Identified an Honest Broker who will agree to meet with you on a scheduled, regular basis (weekly, bi-weekly, or monthly) to discuss what has happened up to this point, what you would like to see happen next in your career, and how best to make it happen. (We'll be looking closely at how to identify, select and work with an Honest Broker in the next few chapters of this book.)

* Created and analyzed a written 16-28 Narrative with your Honest Broker. (We'll examine how to do that, too.)

* Created and analyzed a Career Options Wheel and an Action Plan, each based on what you learn, with your Honest Broker's help, from your 16 - 28 Narrative. (These two steps, too, will be covered in detail.)

Until you've done all of that, don't rush to fill in the blanks. Let the blanks be. Don't pretend that you know what comes next, even if someone you love seems to think that you should. Work with someone you trust and respect. Ask that person to help you learn to listen carefully to all that has come before ... and to take careful note of all the clues you hear about what might be coming next.

*I absolutely believe that people, unless coached, never reach their maximum capabilities.—Bob Nardelli, former CEO, Home Depot*

You should not expect to be able to handle this process entirely on your own. You will need a sounding board, someone who will challenge you, listen to you, encourage you, help you to connect the dots, and pose questions that you may have overlooked. You will need, in short, an Honest Broker

The Honest Broker Should Be...

16-28: Unleash the Passions of Your Youth...

13

* Willing to serve as your facilitator, as the poser of important career-related and life-related questions you may have overlooked – not as your boss, or your therapist, or your codependent.

* Not related to you by blood.

* Not connected to you in any recurring social context other than the Honest Broker role. (In other words, don't pick your best friend; do pick someone like a workplace colleague you respect, but don't go out to the movies with.)

* Accessible to you at any (reasonable) time by phone for brainstorming and/or reality checks.

* Willing to take part in regularly scheduled face-to-face meetings for 45 - 90 minutes without interruptions (including telephone calls). These meetings should take place weekly, bi-weekly, or monthly, and should be in both your calendar and the Honest Broker's calendar.

* Empathetic, non-judgmental, and willing to listen to you at length. (This turns out to be much more important to the success of your cause than deep experience within your so-called "target industry," in part because the result of your conversations be to focus on a different "target industry" than the one you initially consider.)

* Enjoyable for you to talk to. (This is non-negotiable. If you don't actually enjoy interacting with this person about what has happened to you in your adolescence and young adulthood, what has happened to you in your adult career, and what could happen next, you should not select that person as your Honest Broker.)

* Willing to read this book.

16-28: Unleash the Passions of Your Youth...

14

* Wise. (This, too, is non-negotiable. I'll explain exactly what I mean by "wise," and share my favorite role model for wisdom, in the next section.)

## The Wise King

*"I'd rather regret the things I've done than regret the things I haven't done." — Lucille Ball*

I just told you that you are looking for wisdom in your Honest Broker. I define "wisdom" in this role as "the ability to help you reveal who you truly are ... so you can make better choices as a result."

Many people have intelligence. Very few people are wise enough to pose the kinds of questions that illuminate exactly what should happen next in someone's life. It's nice to have an Honest Broker who's intelligent and has lots of experience within an industry that you think is right for you ... but if you have to choose between someone who has broad experience in a certain industry and someone who offers the wisdom that helps you to determine whether or not that industry is even right for you, I hope you choose the wisdom.

Let me give you my favorite example of the kind of wisdom I'm talking about. It's an old story. You may have heard it before. It has to do with a king who lived long ago, a king who was presented with a seemingly impossible decision.

> (T)wo prostitutes came to the king and stood before him. The one woman said, "Oh, my lord, this woman and I live in the same house, and I gave birth to a child while she was in the house. Then on the third day after I gave birth,

16-28: Unleash the Passions of Your Youth…

15

this woman also gave birth. And we were alone. There was no one else with us in the house; only we two were in the house. And this woman's son died in the night, because she lay on him. And she arose at midnight and took my son from beside me, while your servant slept, and laid him at her breast, and laid her dead son at my breast. When I rose in the morning to nurse my child, behold, he was dead. But when I looked at him closely in the morning, behold, he was not the child that I had borne." But the other woman said, "No, the living child is mine, and the dead child is yours." The first said, "No, the dead child is yours, and the living child is mine." Thus they spoke before the king.

Then the king said, "The one says, 'This is my son that is alive, and your son is dead'; and the other says, 'No; but your son is dead, and my son is the living one.'" And the king said, "Bring me a sword." So a sword was brought before the king. And the king said, "Divide the living child in two, and give half to the one and half to the other."

Then the woman whose son was alive said to the king, because her heart yearned for her son, "Oh, my lord, give her the living child, and by no means put him to death." But the other said, "He shall be neither mine nor yours; divide him." Then the king answered and said, "Give the living child to the first woman, and by no means put him to death; she is his mother." And all Israel heard of the judgment that the king had

16-28: Unleash the Passions of Your Youth...

rendered, and they stood in awe of the king, because they perceived that the wisdom of God was in him to do justice.

The king was Solomon, and he knew how to get to the bottom of things. Notice what Solomon did: he pushed people in an unexpected way. He provoked people. He sparked an emotional reaction that revealed who was really who.

While you (probably) won't be asking your Honest Broker to decide matters of life, death, and motherhood, you will be counting on him or her to provoke you a little bit, to ask uncomfortable questions, and to spark an emotional reaction that reveals who you really are.

One of the chief tools the Honest Broker will be using is *The 16-28 Solution-Unleash the Passions of Your Youth: Five Big Lessons to ReIgnite Your Career.* This is a simple approach that allows you to harness the immense power of your own personal history in helping you to identify who you really are and what you ought to consider doing next. It's a tool most people at a career crossroads overlook. It's a tool that your Honest Broker will be using throughout this process to challenge you, provoke you, and spark the emotional reaction that identifies where your true aptitudes and passions lie.

16-28: Unleash the Passions of Your Youth…

## Case I: The Turning Point
## Youth … and Emerging Adulthood Lesson
## One: Find Your Compass Point
### I: The Crossroads

*Desperation is the raw material of drastic change. —
William S. Burroughs*

Mike was in his mid-fifties when he realized that he wanted out.

He had spent over twenty years of his life working as a senior global executive for one of the largest financial services companies in the world. It was the kind of job people simply didn't leave … unless they had to. And for some reason that he himself found hard to articulate, Mike had concluded that he had to leave.

Mike had the kind of career track "goodies" that nearly all people in his industry envied: a seven-figure salary, an intricate, generous bonus package that kicked in just about every year, great benefits, and a long list of similar perks. And that career track was headed for nothing but blue skies ahead — in financial terms, at least — when Mike scheduled a face-to-face meeting with the senior executive in his department.

Personally, however, Mike knew he was deeply tired of it all: tired of the politicking, the infighting, the cliques, the numbing familiarity of what he spent most every day doing — and tired, too, of something else, something he was having a hard time putting his finger on, something in his work that no longer matched up with who he had set out to be. The feeling of there being a profound mismatch had been getting harder and harder for him to shake.

16-28: Unleash the Passions of Your Youth…

So it was, one morning, that he sat down in the executive's office and announced that he had decided it was time to part ways and for Mike to move on, that he was grateful to have been part of the organization, that he wanted a smooth transition, and that it was time to negotiate an exit package.

The executive — who knew all the signs of someone who has made up his mind — accepted Mike's decision and didn't challenge it in any way. He said he was sorry to see Mike go. He thanked Mike for his willingness to set a lengthy timeline before his departure, and for his offer to help oversee the transition, which was immediately accepted. The executive did have one question, though — the same one that Mike had been rolling over and over in his own head.

What was next for him?

Mike didn't know. He knew he wanted to leave, but that was about all he knew, which explains how he and I came to meet.

## II: Where to Go From Here

*"Whatever sorrow shakes from your heart, far better things will take their place."* — *Rumi*

"This is a personal decision first, and an economic one second," Mike told me near the beginning of our first meeting. That sentence not only drove most of the first session ... it stayed with me for weeks. It encapsulated so many other discussions with so many other people who had worked with me in the past.

That's the way it is for most of my clients: They establish, and come to terms with, the personal priorities of "where to go from here" ... and then they take a look at the economic options This is, in my experience, a formula for sound decision making in the

16-28: Unleash the Passions of Your Youth...

area of career management, especially for people who find themselves at a career crossroads after the age of forty. They make it a personal decision first.

This is not to say that economic issues are nonexistent or irrelevant to the people who decide to work with me. There are financial challenges to consider, sometimes quite serious ones. But the whole point of the work we do together is to find the reliable internal compass that establishes a "where to go from here" destination that engages with the person on a deep emotional level ... and makes the financial decisions more likely to be successful ones in both the short and the long terms.

Mike's employer had arranged for him to meet with me so we could develop a customized transition plan together. My role would be the same for him as it would be for each of my clients: to serve as a coach.

> ***A "career crossroads" is any major career decision that you face.***

I told Mike at the outset of that very first session that he should expect me to do a lot more listening than talking, especially during our first couple of meetings. He nodded and agreed that this was a good idea. Then I asked him to share, to the best of his ability, what had led him to leave the company he had served so faithfully for so long. He leaned back, gave a long sigh ... and then began.

## III: A Changing World

*"When you fight yourself to discover the real you, there is only one winner." — Stephen Richards*

16-28: Unleash the Passions of Your Youth…

"There had been a big cultural change at the company over the last few years," Mike said, with just a trace of sadness in his voice. "I know that what I'm about to say might sound a little strange to someone who is not used to thinking about a financial services company this way, but it's still true: We were a family, and we looked out for each other, and we looked out for the consumer."

I nodded and made a mental note of the word "family," which seemed to carry special significance for Mike. He had emphasized it with great force, his voice nearly breaking.

"The reality is that there were a whole lot of careers and a whole lot of alliances over there that had been built around the principle of helping each other and helping our customers. And when the new regime came in, that value of helping each other just wasn't a driving message from the top of the organization, the way it had been before. I don't want you to think we weren't trying to improve our bottom line in the years before the new CEO came on. We certainly were. But there was a different culture to deal with under the new leadership team, a culture that was less collaborative, less respectful, less concerned with supporting relationships, less like ..."

He left the sentence unfinished and stared out the window for a long moment.

"Like family?" I offered.

"Yes. Precisely," he said. "Like family." He kept staring at the windowpane, and then continued. "There was one morning when I was getting out of the car in the parking lot and saying out loud 'I hate going in here.' I never use the word 'hate!' I looked around quickly to see if anyone heard me, and then went in to the

16-28: Unleash the Passions of Your Youth...

office. That was a sign to me that there had been a serious disconnect somewhere along the line. That was the first sign that something needed to change, that I was no longer in the right place."

"How did that feel?" I asked.

"It felt scary at first. It felt like a challenge to the status quo. I had been working there for a long, long, time. But it also felt like reality to admit that it was time to move on."

## IV: The Compass

*"Did they know why they knew? Not at all. But they Knew!" — Malcolm Gladwell*

Mike's strong response to the impossible-to-ignore change in workplace culture at his long-time employer — "I was no longer in the right place" — was distinctive to him as an individual. It was deeply rooted in his own direct life experience. It was a reaction to a critical directional shift in his circumstances, a shift made obvious to him by his own internal personal compass. We each have a compass like that, a compass that tells each of us what feels right and what feels wrong on an individual level about our own career choices.

The thing about internal compasses is that they only work for one person. Others working at that same global company over a similar or the same time span could have chosen, and indeed did choose, to stay on. For Mike, though, the alarm bells went off, and once they did, he made a change.

To his credit, Mike concluded that it didn't really matter whether the change he decided he had to make (and could not yet describe) made sense to someone else. Most people would have

16-28: Unleash the Passions of Your Youth…

wondered why in the world a man at the top of his career, highly regarded within the industry of his own choosing, and earning a substantial salary, would opt to walk away and start all over again.

The internal compass that compelled Mike to make a change was calibrated to something important and unique about his own personal life history. That compass was and is connected to a period from his late adolescence and early adulthood that I call the 16 - 28 window.

Events, emotions, experiences, and aptitudes from that critical formative period in our lives are, I believe, what cause the alarm bells to go off for us whenever our careers reach important points of transition ... and they are also what allow us to heed these alarm bells in a way that can eventually allow us identify our own right next step.

## V: Family

*"It is not flesh and blood but the heart which makes us fathers and sons." — Johann Schiller*

There was an important, sensitive piece of personal history that came out of my early sessions with Mike, an important bit of backstory that not only helped to explain a lot of what had happened to change his feelings about his workplace, but also helped us to identify the right next step for him, the right North on his personal compass. This backstory emerged during examination of the fateful period of Mike's life that occurred between the ages of sixteen and twenty-eight.

> **The years between sixteen and twenty-eight, and especially the experiences that inspired us and led us to our**

16-28: Unleash the Passions of Your Youth…

23

*earliest workplace passions during those years, often contain important clues about what we should do with our lives when we reach a career crossroads.*

The backstory was this: Mike's early home life was quite difficult. In fact, his adolescence and young adulthood was what many of us would have classified as troubled, and his path out of that dysfunctional family situation was a rocky one. At about the age of seventeen, he took a turn toward a local religious community, a local Protestant denomination that supported him and sustained him through some very tough times. Within that worship community, he found a mentor-like figure — I'll call him Dan — who assumed a pseudo-parental role. Dan's family welcomed Mike, who was at that point a troubled teen whose life could have gone in any number of painful directions. Instead, it went in a very good direction.

*A "mentor" is a wise and trusted counselor or teacher.*

And the reason Mike's life went in a good direction (he believed, and I had no reason to dispute) — the reason he had been able to study for and launch a great career in the industry of his choice — the reason he had been able to succeed in that industry — all came down to one simple word: 'Family."

## VI: Many Options

*"Often people attempt to live their lives backwards: They try to have more things, or more money, in order to do more of what they want so that they will be happier. The way it actually works is the reverse. You must first be who*

16-28: Unleash the Passions of Your Youth…

*you really are, then, do what you need to do, in order to
have what you want."—Margaret Young*

In hindsight, it would be easy to make the mistake of assuming
that there was one and only one obviously right career path for
Mike — the one that we eventually settled on. But the truth, as it
usually is, was a little more complex than that. There were many
options for us to discuss, as you would expect in the case of a
major executive leaving a Fortune 100 company after twenty
plus years of experience that included substantial experience in
strategic planning, product development, brand innovation, and
national and international marketing.

There were a lot of doors for us to consider knocking on, and a
lot of opportunities to consider. Our challenge was not really to
create or find new opportunities (as it had been with other clients
I'd worked with), but rather to create a short list from a much
longer list of possible next steps. Mike wanted to take, not any
next step, but the right next step for him. And he was looking to
me for help in identifying the right tools, the tools that would
help him to narrow his field and set the right priorities, the
priorities that best reflected him at this stage of his life.

In a very real sense, Mike and I were discussing, not just career
management strategy, but life management strategies.

To do that, we had to look closely at just about everything of
significance that had come before in his life — not just over the
past ten or fifteen years, but also in the years of his adolescence
and young adulthood. Once we identified the key themes, we
could see how they might help us to revise his list of five or six
options down to a more manageable list of two or three.

16-28: Unleash the Passions of Your Youth…

In evaluating Mike's own assessments of his life and career, as well as the input of others who had lived with him, worked with him, and shown an eagerness to help him find the right move forward, I noticed that there were a number of themes came up again and again in our discussions. They were:

* Ethics

* Community

* Values

* Leadership

* Family

I asked Mike if he was willing to build our Short List around the opportunities that seemed to him most likely to support these themes – which were also, it turned out, important elements in the spiritual life that had sustained him for over three decades.

"Great idea," he said. "Let's get started."

## VII: Avoid the Rush to Decide "What's Next?"

*"He that can have patience can have what he will."* — *Benjamin Franklin*

What I want you to notice at this point is that Mike and I invested our time in a number of extremely important steps before we even thought about trying to identify the best answer to the question "What's next?"

Although that question is definitely an important one, my experience is that rushing to find an answer for it does not

16-28: Unleash the Passions of Your Youth…

always serve the person who finds himself or herself at a career crossroads. Instead of attempting to come up with an instant, plausible response to the common question of (well-intentioned) friends and loved ones, "So — what are you going to do now?" I want to urge you to build up the courage necessary to make the honest reply, "I'm still working on that."

## VIII: The Unexpected Gift

*"The fate of your heart is your choice and in that fate no one else gets a vote" — Sarah Dessen*

Two of the three full-time opportunities we had decided to pursue at top-tier possibilities — an opening as an executive director at the church where he was a member, and a job as the senior financing director at a local housing non-profit — were now on the short list. They were there not only because of direct connections that Mike had made in the weeks since we had begun our sessions, but also because of their strong resonance with the themes of Ethics, Community, Values, Leadership, and Family we had identified. These were ideas we had examined at length in conversation, and they were strong emotional touch points that Mike explored more fully is his 16 - 28 Narrative (a document whose purpose and structure we'll examine in the next chapter). The point is, the central event of Mike's 16 - 28 Narrative turned out to be a challenging one. He had had grown up in a troubled family, and decided to leave home at an early age.

How was that event a benefit to our process? Well, it was a turning point in Mike's life. Such turning points often yield important insights about our core values and interests, especially when they take place in the late teens or early twenties. These values and interests can be especially important later on in life,

16-28: Unleash the Passions of Your Youth...

27

when we are looking for guidance, reminders, and insights about what should come next in our career. It's quite common, however, for us to lose touch with the values and interests that helped us to forge and test our adult identities. We get distracted. We forget. That's the whole reason we want to engage with an Honest Broker: not to tell us things we don't know about ourselves and our path, but to help us to reconnect with the things we already do know, but may have lost sight of temporarily.

When he left home to escape from a chaotic and dysfunctional domestic environment, Mike came under the protection of the pastor of a local church. The pastor listened to Mike's story and decided to help. As it happened, he ran a shelter for at-risk youth, and he emerged as an important mentor figure for Mike. The church community became, for Mike, a kind of second family, a family built on pillars that would sustain and support Mike in his adult life: responsibility, giving back, and the establishment of a "safe place."

This desire to create and maintain a safe place turned out to be one of the driving forces of Mike's whole career. The feeling that there he could create an organizational commitment to maintain a safe place — a place where people could be supported as though they were members of the family — was a major motivator during the long period of his career that had unfolded at the company. But the takeover of the company by a new regime, a takeover that had begun with the word that senior management would soon be implementing layoffs and budget cuts, had made Mike deeply uncomfortable, and had sent him into a feeling of not belonging there anymore. Now, having completed his 16 - 28 Narrative, he knew why. The removal of his own ability to maintain a safe place, a place that let people feel as supported as they would if they were family — maybe

16-28: Unleash the Passions of Your Youth…

even more supported — set off an alarm. That company was no longer what Mike was all about. It had been once, but that had changed.

The challenges of Mike's youth and young adulthood, which had been a painful experience, had led him to something constructive. He had used the negative experience to establish a positive adult identity. Now that he had uncovered the roots of that identity (with the help of an Honest Broker, me), creating the Short List of opportunities that made both financial and emotional sense — not to anyone else, but to him — became a lot easier. The formative experience of his young adulthood — losing one home, and creating another — turned out to be an unexpected gift. He had the compass he needed to navigate his own career crossroads successfully.

## IX: The Career Options Wheel

*"To map out a course of action and follow it to an end requires some of the same courage that a soldier needs. Peace has its victories, but it takes brave men and women to win them." — Ralph Waldo Emerson*

At various points in our discussions, Mike and I would arrange all of what he currently considered his A list opportunities into a visual brainstorming display that I call a Career Options Wheel. Basically, this is a diagram of your best current options. There's a central circle representing you, the person who's trying to figure out what comes next in his or her professional life — in this case, the central circle read "Mike" — and that circle in the middle is surrounded by a group of outer circles, each of which are connected back to the circle in the middle by a line. The

16-28: Unleash the Passions of Your Youth...

29

larger the outer circle is, the more attractive the potential opportunity is to the person whose name appears in the middle.

These maps are not binding in any way; they just give you a snapshot image of where you think you are and what you are now looking at pursuing with the greatest level of enthusiasm. You can create a Career Choices Map at any stage of the process we're talking about, but in my experience they tend to be more meaningful and more useful once you have created the 16 - 28 Narrative that gets you closer to understanding what True North is for you as a person.

It's often quite interesting to compare early Career Options Wheels with later ones. During the first few weeks of my discussions with Mike, before he had completed his 16-28 Narrative, his very first Career Options Wheel looked like this:

Notice that the opportunity with the highest potential salary occupies the largest circle. This was a function of Mike applying a set of standards that had more to do with the expectations of other people than it did with him deciding where he wanted to go next in his life. As a practical matter, Mike was quite well off; he had ample resources after his long years of service with the company. (One of the early breakthroughs in our discussions came when Mike reached the conclusion that he did not have to make his next career move based on financial considerations.)

Once we had identified Mike's True North orientation, two or three weeks later, and once Mike had applied the takeaways from his 16 - 28 Narrative to an evaluation if his Short List, he created a Career Options Wheel that looked like this:

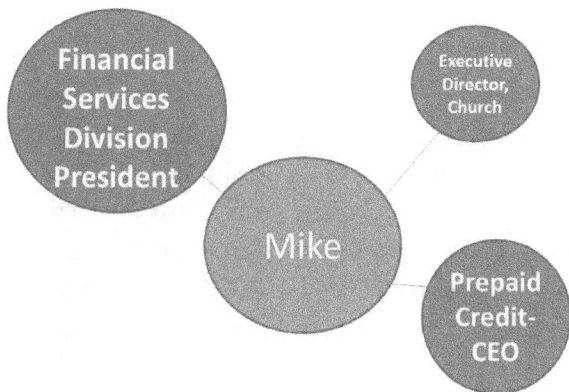

## X: The Right Move

*"None are so old as those who have outlived enthusiasm."*— *Henry David Thoreau*

Over the course of a number of weeks, Mike and I were able to use our sessions together to leverage the experiences of his late adolescence and young adulthood in a powerful way.

16-28: Unleash the Passions of Your Youth…

By chronicling those experiences, examining them closely, and identifying the lessons that they showed us about how Mike had responded to an important early challenge in his life, we were able to draw some conclusions. Specifically, we were able to identify what remained central in Mike's continually revised understanding of himself and his mission in the workplace. Just as important, we were able to get some clarity about what motivated him, what left him feeling passionate, engaged, and committed -- and what didn't.

Over and over again, I have found, in working with my clients, that the 16 - 28 coaching process that I am describing here is one of the most reliable tools for determining what someone is likely to become excited about. Experience — not just my own — has also shown that focusing someone's attentions on a career path for which he or she has little or no personal enthusiasm is a losing gambit, no matter how successful that career path may appear to someone else. Experience has also shown that, once someone has connected with a career option that truly resonates with him or her, it can deliver extraordinary rewards, no matter how unlikely or uninspiring that option may seem to someone else.

This is how it was for Mike. His former colleagues at the financial services company probably would never have imagined that he could have considered himself successful working as the executive director of a well-known church in Fairfield, Connecticut — leading, managing and caring for the church's staff, supporting its outreach work in various ministries (including work with young people in troubled family situations), and reporting to a group of church elders — all at a fraction of his former salary. The reason they could not have seen the success in this choice, however, was that they had a different True North than Mike did.

Mike's True North lay in creating a safe place, a home, a shelter, for people who were in need. That's what we learned together, not only by examining his 16 - 28 Narrative, but also by examining the rest of his career. (The parts of his financial services career that he had found most rewarding, for instance, usually involved mentorship and the development of younger staff members.) This instinct tied in powerfully to Mike's 16 - 28 experiences, of course. Gaining an understanding of his own True North instinct gave Mike a deeper confidence in pursuing it, even though the job he ended up taking was not what a lot of people in his circle expected from him. He didn't care. The very idea of it energized him. And now he knew why.

His wife understood. He understood. And that was enough. He accepted the executive director position at the church, and he hasn't looked back since.

It was the right move.

## Case II: Bouncing Back
## Youth ... and Emerging Adulthood Lesson Two: Identify Core Strengths That Allow You to Make Breakthrough Contributions
### XI: Juan's Passion, Juan's Challenge

*"One can never consent to creep when one feels an impulse to soar."* — *Helen Keller,* The Story of My Life

I probably never would have ended up working with Juan had it not been for two fortuitous circumstances: a shared interest in sports, and a long restaurant discussion about what he felt wasn't working in his career.

Juan is one of those clients who started out as a social acquaintance, and has remained a good friend. I met him, and struck up my first conversation with him, thanks to an accident of our dinner seating arrangements. He bought a house from a friend of mine who had invited both of us out to celebrate their recent purchase and move to town. Juan sat next to me, and he lit up like a Christmas tree when I happened to mention that I followed college athletics. As it happens, I had stumbled onto Juan's great passion in life: He had played sports as a youngster in Mexico, in college at Virginia, and even put in a season and a half at the professional level in Canada. He worked in the marketing department of a U.S. professional sports league.

Juan and I, fortuitous seat-mates, discussed the performance of the local college teams for a period of time that must have been an hour, but that seemed like about ten minutes. He was a great conversationalist. I was impressed by his love of sport, his deep knowledge of it, and his ability to adapt his own experience and insights to include those of a dinner partner who knew far less

16-28: Unleash the Passions of Your Youth...

about athletics than he did. I remember thinking that he was one of the most approachable, passionate people I'd ever met.

But the mood changed the minute I asked him to tell me how things were going at his job. Apparently there were problems on the career front, because my buoyant, accessible, and enthusiastic seat-mate turned instantly morose and dejected when he began talking about his supervisor.

Something was definitely wrong here. I was curious to find out just what it was.

## XII: The Carl Principle

Juan explained to me after dessert that when it came to his career, he found himself walking down a blind alley.

He had thought that a set of white collar responsibilities that connected to the game he loved would have been a dream come true, a chance to connect on a person-to-person basis with players, with owners, with management, and even with fans who shared his dream: to expand the national and global profile of his sport. Instead, he found himself stuck in a very different situation, a hierarchical game whose rules he only dimly understood.

Juan reported directly to the Executive Vice President of Marketing, a man named Carl. Carl was schooled first and foremost in the game of internal company politics, and he played it well. There was nothing wrong with this in and of itself, but he was stifling Juan. Naturally gregarious, Juan was the kind of person who derives energy from connecting with other people. He had a lot of ideas. And he had a lot of enthusiasm. But Carl had him on a very short leash. He insisted that all of his communications with anyone else in the company (or outside of

16-28: Unleash the Passions of Your Youth...

35

it, for that matter) be cleared through him. He liked to keep him within a couple of hundred feet of his office. And Carl had an unfortunate habit of taking Juan's ideas, putting his name on them, and claiming personal credit for them.

Carl was (from all I could make out) a perfect representative of what management experts called The Peter Principle — that is, someone who had been risen to his own personal level of incompetence. I thought it was extremely unlikely that he would ever rise to play a major role within the league, or any other professional organization, because of what appeared to be some glaring deficits in his leadership profile. According to Juan, whose account I trusted, he was not good at spotting or developing talent, felt threatened by the creativity of others, and made questionable ethical choices. Juan was particularly bitter about his habit of taking credit for Juan's work and innovative ideas, but he didn't have any clear sense about how he could change the situation. He felt trapped.

At the end of the evening, we made an appointment for him to stop by my office and see me for a formal counseling session.

## XII: The Sophomore Crisis

*"Sometimes you need a little crisis to get your adrenaline flowing and help you realize your potential."* — *Jeannette Walls,* The Glass Castle

The next week, I began to get the whole story.

Juan had enjoyed a very successful college career. He went to The University of Virginia (UVA) on an athletic scholarship, and he quickly made the varsity team. In the span of a single year, he had moved from being a well-regarded teenaged jock in Mexico

16-28: Unleash the Passions of Your Youth...

to being a big man on campus at one of the world's great universities. In fact, he had been a little surprised at how quickly he emerged as a star player on the University of Virginia squad. However, unlike some of the other star players, Juan was committed to the goal of posting high grades and securing a meaningful degree during his college years.

Juan was determined to build a real career for himself, to set himself up for something that went beyond his talents on the field, which, though, considerable, were not reflective of everything he could do. He was a promising math student and (some said) a born salesperson. He wanted a future, and he expected to earn one at UVA.

He was a little taken aback, though, by how just much work that entailed. Juan felt as though his freshman year went by in a blur: a blur of practices, of classes, of home games, of sleepless nights worrying about final exams. The team did well, and he did well, but at the end of his first year in school, he wasn't happy with his academic performance. He was a star athlete, but he was one of those star athletes who was barely keeping his head above water academically, and that's not what he had come to UVA to do.

He wasn't sure how he would be able to keep up in his sophomore year, when he knew his course load would be much heavier. Over the summer, he reached out to his favorite professor, a Dr. Jamison. Dr. Jamison had taught an entry-level sociology course he had loved — although he had hoped for more than the C he earned in that class. Juan phoned him in early August and asked him for some help in making sense of his insane, seemingly impossible schedule. How could he possibly earn the grades he wanted, and felt he deserved, with all the away games he had coming up, and all the courses he wanted to

16-28: Unleash the Passions of Your Youth...

37

take? What could Juan do to avoid an academic crisis in his sophomore year?

The conversation that followed was, as they say, the beginning of a beautiful friendship.

## XIII: The Mentor

*"Tell me and I forget, teach me and I may remember, involve me and I learn."* — *Benjamin Franklin*

Dr. Jamison — who had been a college athlete himself — was more than happy to help.

Over the phone, and via e-mail, Dr. Jamison set up a brand-new time management system for Juan. He urged him to prioritize all of his assignments, so that he would be able to work first and foremost on the ones that had the highest potential impact on his grade. That was a new idea; up to this point, Juan had simply been tackling the assignments in the order in which he had received them. Dr. Jamison wanted him to set up a battle plan first.

What was more, he wanted Juan to play to his strengths. Having been instructed for his whole life that he should finish one thing before starting another, especially in regard to school assignments, Juan was surprised to hear Dr. Jamison inform him that some people had a very different working style. Some people worked best in small bursts and thrived on interruptions. Dr. Jamison knew himself to be such a person, and he suspected Juan to be such a person as well. He encouraged Juan to read and write as long as he felt interest in a topic, and to switch channels between two assignments, rather than trying to push forward relentlessly with one assign for two or three hours at a time. Juan had never thought of himself as being particularly good at setting

16-28: Unleash the Passions of Your Youth…

38

priorities or following systems, but something told him that this new way of working was going to a lot easier to use than his previous mode of working. It would allow him to get his work done in a way that made the most sense to him and made the most of his limited attention span. Dr. Jamison assured him that his own attention span was just as narrow.

Just as important as either of these changes, Dr. Jamison showed Juan how to negotiate with his professors. In situations where he needed a little extra time to complete assignment because of an away game, Dr. Jamison encouraged Juan to interact proactively with the professor and ask for an extension. This had never even occurred to Juan.

Another thing that surprised Juan was that Dr. Jamison made sure the weekly schedule included enough downtime for him to feel as though he weren't being rushed and stressed for all of his waking hours. He would still have time to hang out with his friends. Not as much time as he had during his freshman year, perhaps but enough to make him feel like there was a reward for all of his hard work.

When he first heard all the details of this new system, Juan instantly felt more motivated and less stressed. He also felt very grateful to Dr. Jamison, and he looked forward to taking his next sociology class.

Two remarkable things happened during Juan's sophomore year at the University of Virginia. The first was that the new time management system worked. It was amazingly easy to implement, and task management during Juan's sophomore year turned out to be much easier than he had anticipated. It had not been a crisis. Sure, he worked hard, both on and off the field, but he had attained his goals. He had a great season with the team, and he had learned how to manage his own workflow. He

16-28: Unleash the Passions of Your Youth…

finished that year with a grade point average of 3.75. Perhaps just as important, he finished that year with a solid professional relationship with a mentor whom he respected deeply, someone who wanted to see him make the most of himself. The summer following his sophomore year, Juan kept on working informally, via e-mail, with Dr. Jamison, who opened his eyes not only to the world of sociology, but also to subjects as diverse as international relations, literature, and art history.

Juan had found his mentor.

## XIV: Two Pieces of Bad News

*"Unseen in the background, Fate was quietly slipping lead into the boxing-glove."* — *P.G. Wodehouse*

Juan graduated from the University of Virginia with honors. It was quite an accomplishment! His parents came to the graduation ceremony, all the way from Mexico. Dr. Jamison was there, too, of course. After the ceremony, they all went out for a celebratory dinner and toasted the good news that had just been confirmed that very morning: Juan had received an offer to play professionally. He would be turning pro in a matter of months.

Dr. Jamison was excited, just as his parents were excited ..., but the good doctor, who had grown used to meeting with Juan two days a week to share advice that Juan followed but didn't always want to hear, urged him to take a moment to reflect. Over dinner, Dr. Jamison urged Juan to consider the importance of balancing his life a little more carefully. An athlete's career was short. A life of the mind, of social connection, of aspiration, of achievement in the realms of business or art or science, would last much longer and be much more satisfying in the long run. He urged Juan to develop a backup plan. Perhaps he would

16-28: Unleash the Passions of Your Youth...

40

consider a one-year break before starting his pro career? Just to find his footing professionally?

Juan promised that he would think about that, but in all the hustle and preparation for his first year as a pro, he never really did. He could hardly be blamed: He was about to embark on the adventure of a lifetime, an athlete's adventure. He neglected to follow through on Dr. Jamison's advice, and he ignored the creation of his backup plan. He got caught up in the excitement of the moment. He began doing something he had never done in college, namely: fixating on sports to the exclusion of all else.

It would be nice to report that Juan had a stellar rookie year as a pro, but the truth as it played out in Juan's life that year proved much more difficult for all concerned. He struggled that season, as he had never struggled on the field. Juan found himself competing against a level of talent that he simply hadn't encountered during his high school or college years. He injured himself badly halfway through the season. It was a knee injury, a serious one. It would take six months to recover from. After having compiled mediocre statistics at best for the first half of the season, Juan found himself cut from the team. Worse news yet came within just a month of that depressing development.

Dr. Jamison, Juan learned from a college friend, had died of a sudden heart attack.

## XV: An Opportunity

*"Shallow men believe in luck or in circumstance. Strong men believe in cause and effect." — Ralph Waldo Emerson*

16-28: Unleash the Passions of Your Youth…

41

The news of his mentor's death troubled Juan greatly, and was one of the reasons the next year was so difficult for him. The year seemed to slip by in a haze.

He liked to tell his friends that he was going through a transitional period,. In truth, he knew that that word "transitional" was nothing more than a euphemism. He had not yet regained his footing since being cut from the team and the league, and the man who had always been there to offer him good advice was no longer there to consult. He had not the slightest sense of what to do next. His finances looked worse with each passing week. But the money wasn't the real problem, he knew. The true difficulty, he sensed, was that he was feeling low about himself. Why? Because his career as a professional athlete had ended quickly and unexpectedly, just as Dr. Jamison had warned that it would. He had wanted much more from that career. Now that it was over, he simply did not know where to go next in his life. Juan felt the inevitable depression of a gifted athlete who is no longer allowed to perform on the field in his sport of choice, but he also felt something else, something deeper: a sense that his best talents lay undiscovered and were not being put to use. The sense that he was wasting time depressed him, and caused him to waste more of it.

Juan drifted from job to job, working part-time through a temp agency at assignments that bored him, assisted with coaching a few hours a week at a local high school, and helping out family and friends with handyman and fix-up work. He was pursuing no definite career goal. His parents could tell that he was in a rut. And so could his friends.

A former teammate of his, by the name of Roger, took them out to lunch one day and tried to lift his spirits. Hadn't he spent enough time wandering in the wilderness? Hadn't he picked up a

16-28: Unleash the Passions of Your Youth...

hunger to make something more of himself during his college years? Didn't he owe it to himself, and to those who loved him and were counting on him, to find something newer and bigger and better to pursue in his life?

Jay appreciated the talk, and told his friend Roger he would heed his advice and begin the search for a new career. After a weekend doing some research in the Internet, as well as some research into his own heart, he decided to focus on marketing, as that was one of the areas Dr. Jamison had continually suggested to look into, and he began to conduct a real job search. Within four weeks, he reached out to a professional sports league, turned the receptionist there into an ally, secured a lunch meeting with Carl — a former college star like himself — and made his case for a position on his staff. He was, he promised him, someone who could help him to expand the sport they both loved to the national prominence. Someone he could count on. Someone who would make him look good.

Carl offered him a job. It was, his parents said, the lucky break they had all been waiting for.

## XVI: Just Another Horse in the Stable

Up to this point, Juan had been fortunate to work mostly under the care of coaches who cared deeply for him. He had been blessed, in fact, to have worked with coaches who, every step of the way, actually had Juan's best interests in mind. He had had three good coaches during his middle school and high school playing career in Mexico, and he had had a good mentor in Dr. Jamison. Even his coach in the pro league had been supportive and helpful, and had taken the time to help Juan come to terms with what turned out to be a career-ending injury.

16-28: Unleash the Passions of Your Youth…

43

But Carl was his first real boss. And a boss, Juan learned very quickly, can be very different from a coach.

Carl had said all the right words during the interview and the on-boarding process. He talked about wanting Juan to succeed, about how important it was for him to expand his horizons, about how he had to continue his education and stretch himself with new goals, goals that gave him a feeling of inspiration and possibility, about how the sky was the limit for him. But although he said all those things, his actions, Juan learned very quickly, simply did not match up with the words. In fact they tended to go in precisely the opposite direction.

Juan's first few weeks on the job had been uneventful, and as he'd settled in, he had certainly gotten the sense that Carl was (as he frequently pointed out) there for him to consult should he ever need consultation. But he soon realized that the daily support and interaction he had grown used to in school and on the team was now a thing of the past. He was on his own, and if he wanted feedback or guidance, he wasn't going to get that — or much of anything else — on a daily basis from Carl.

Once a week, Carl would have a one-on-one meeting with him, and explore various ideas he had come up with for promoting the league. Most of them Carl dismissed instantly as "stupid." Juan was not used to this kind of dismissive, not to say disrespectful, attitude, and he was not sure how to respond to it. But there was no one to ask for advice no one to share the new rules of the game that he was playing.

Every week, Carl told him to keep pushing, keep researching, keep coming up with new ideas. This he did.

After about a month or so on the job, after Juan could had completed his orientation and met everyone of consequence in

16-28: Unleash the Passions of Your Youth...

the organization, and after he had put his time in to learn what the fans wanted and how they saw the games they were attending, Juan came up with what he thought was a brilliant idea. It was based on the interviews with fans that he had conducted.

The idea involved using social media to engage attendees at matches and inspire them to make live comments during the game to their friends. The outlay of capital was minimal, and the results achieved by similar initiatives in other sports had been very impressive.

Carl liked the idea. He liked so much in fact, that he stripped Juan's name from it, added a semicolon or two, placed his own name at the top of the title page, and submitted it to Mark Angelo, the president of the league, as though it were his own.

Mark loved it.

Juan kept his mouth shut, but he boiled with resentment. During a discussion with a colleague, Juan was assured that he had not been the only one who had been treated this way. Once you became a horse in Carl's stable, the colleague explained, you "ran the race and let the jockey claim the victory." That was "just how it worked" in her department. The jockey got all the credit. And the horse got none. No one cared very much about the horse, in fact.

## XVII: Look for the Options

*"Do not despise your own place and hour. Every place is under the stars, every place is the center of the world."* — *John Burroughs,* Studies in Nature and Literature

16-28: Unleash the Passions of Your Youth…

It had gone on like that for several months. Every good idea Juan came up with, Carl found a way to "redesign" superficially and then take all the credit for. Juan told me (during our first session) that he had grown tired of even trying to fit into Carl's world. There was nothing exciting about the job anymore, nothing that felt remotely rewarding, nothing motivating him to wake up each morning and give his best. He was ready to call it quits.

"I'm handing in my resignation letter tomorrow," he said.

I told him I was not quite certain that was the right next step. Not yet, at any rate.

"Why not?" Juan asked.

"Well, for one thing, there's no clear evidence that you've explored all the opportunities at this organization. You love sports. You seem to have a real knack for marketing. You've just inherited a jerk for a boss. That happens. It might make sense for you to move on to another job. Or it might not. Regardless, you are probably better off job hunting from a position of strength, while you're still employed. Before you throw up your hands and walk away, though, which is a step you can't take back, maybe we should think about whether or not there are some other options for you to explore here."

"Other options? What other options could there possibly be?"

That, I explained, was what we had to find out together.

## XVIII: Risk and Reward

*"One opportunity leads directly to another, just as risk leads to more risk, life to more life, and death to more death."* — *Markus Zusak*

16-28: Unleash the Passions of Your Youth…

I asked Juan to tell me about the very best unexplored idea for the league that he had. Was there a breakthrough that, perhaps, he might not have mentioned at work ... because he was concerned that Carl would take credit for it?

He smiled a little sheepishly.

"I see you're grinning now. Presumably there is such an idea?" I asked.

He nodded. "It's something big," he said, "at least potentially. But it's not something I'm willing to have somebody else scribble his name on."

"Well, tell me about it."

Juan proceeded to do so. It was indeed a brilliant idea.

What if, he asked, there were a special fund designed to help the league recruit promising athletes whose careers had started, like his had, outside of the borders of United States?

What if the league focused its recruiting efforts, not just on US colleges, but on targeting and signing the most promising players in the Americas?

What if there was a special investment fund, designed exclusively to provide a signing bonus to the most talented amateur players in North America?

What if the most talented budding players were compensated fairly, even aggressively, in exchange for a multi-year commitment to the league?

What did I think?

I told Juan the truth: The idea sounded pretty promising to me.
16-28: Unleash the Passions of Your Youth...

47

"Who else have you talked about this with?" I asked.

"Nobody," he said.

"Well, I think it's about time for that to change."

"Who can I talk to about it? Remember, I'm still working for Carl. He's my boss."

"So what?" I asked. "He doesn't own you. There's a time and a place to do an end run, Juan," I said, "and you have reached that time and that place. You need to bring this idea up directly to Mark."

## XIX: The Way Forward

*"A ship is safe in harbor, but that's not what ships are for."* — *William G.T. Shedd*

Juan and I spent the better part of an entire one-hour session discussing his reservations about approaching the president of the league directly.

It's worth mentioning here that for him, the rules of the "corporate game" were not at all clear. He had made sense of the college environment, and the environment of the professional athlete, and he had learned how to survive and thrive in his world. Navigating the complexities of office politics, though, was a new and often confusing task. He simply didn't feel comfortable operating in a world he didn't understand.

I asked: "What are the downsides of approaching Mark, the president, with your idea?"

"Directly?"

16-28: Unleash the Passions of Your Youth…

"Directly."

"Well, Carl would get mad," he responded.

"Possible," I said. "Okay. What's the worst case scenario if he gets mad?"

"Well, he might make things difficult for me around the office."

"As far as I can tell, he's making things pretty difficult for you right now."

He agreed that this was the case.

"Anything else?"

"Well, he went on," less certain, "he might try to get me fired."

A silence fell over the room as we both pondered this.

"Let me get this straight," I said, finally. "You're planning to quit the job, but you're afraid that he's going to see to it that you're fired?"

He smiled, and then acknowledged that the reason offered for not taking action was a pretty insubstantial one. "Maybe," he said, "I'm just not used to parting ways with the coach like this. That's what I thought he was going to be, my coach. But it just hasn't worked out."

"Suppose we look at it this way," I said. "Think of the best coach you've ever had. What do you think Dr. Jamison would tell you to do in this situation?"

Juan thought for a moment, then smiled, and said he now knew exactly what he needed to do. We agreed to meet again next week, so he could update me on Mark's response to his idea.

16-28: Unleash the Passions of Your Youth...

## XX: Reward

*"Success is not final, failure is not fatal: it is the courage to continue that counts."* — *Winston Churchill*

When I met with Juan the next week, he was a changed man.

His body language, his facial expression, even the vocabulary he used to describe his work had all turned around 180°. Mark, the CEO, had loved his idea, as did key owners and managers in the league. Mark had been looking for a new way to launch a talent development program within the league, and he loved the idea of bringing an international focus to this important strategic objective.

Faster than anyone, including Juan, had expected, Mark became a major ally. Doors that had seemed shut suddenly opened. What Juan and I had come to call The Carl Saga — management challenges and all — receded into the background. Carl kept a tactful, cautious grin frozen in place during all of the meetings to discuss the program, and all of his interactions with Juan. There had been no conflict, direct or indirect. Carl had simply backed away.

Suddenly, there were negotiations in place to secure a major investment in the player development program. Juan was on the fast track. He was in the right place. And he was enjoying his work again.

I drew two big lessons from my experience with Juan:

First, I saw that many of our 16 - 28 experiences involve a mentor. We can often resolve the career challenges that come

16-28: Unleash the Passions of Your Youth…

along later in life by asking ourselves what that mentor would advise us to do, or how we can best honor his or her example.

And second, I saw that, at every career crossroads, there are usually more options than we imagine. In Juan's case, he had convinced himself that there were absolutely no further opportunities for him in the environment where he was currently working. He was certainly not the first person I'd worked with to walk in the door with that frame of reference. Occasionally, of course, that frame of reference is useful. There are times, however, when it just does not reflect reality.

16-28: Unleash the Passions of Your Youth...

## Case III: Freeing Yourself
## Youth ... and Emerging Adulthood Lesson
## Three: Change What's Not Working
### XXI: Breaking Free

*"This defines entrepreneur and entrepreneurship — the entrepreneur always searches for change, responds to it, and exploits it as an opportunity."* — Peter F. Drucker

Ultimately, understanding your 16 - 28 profile is about learning how you define freedom, and then taking action on that definition.

One of the big lessons I took away from the story I just shared with you is the that, sometimes, it makes a lot of sense to look around your current work environment carefully before you decide it's time to find a new place to make a contribution. There have been many clients I've worked with who walked in the door convinced that there was absolutely no future for them in the organization where they currently worked ... but who found the right opportunity within that company. Sometimes, what needs to change most is inside, rather than outside. For Juan, freedom was waiting to be found in the same company he had once considered a dead end.

Then again, there are plenty of cases where clients have concluded, after careful evaluation, that it really does make sense to move beyond the confines of a working environment where they have spent a fair amount of time. This is particularly true in the case of budding entrepreneurs, many of whom take a few years to figure out their true calling in life. In these situations, a change in scenery really does make the most sense, not just

16-28: Unleash the Passions of Your Youth...

because of adverse conditions in the working environment, but because our aspirations can't possibly be fulfilled within that environment. Some people, I have come to believe, really are cut out to launch their own companies, and are unlikely to find true fulfillment doing anything else. For them, freedom is likely to mean being the boss, rather than reporting to the boss.

In the next section, I'll share one of those stores, the true story of a woman who concluded, after careful analysis, that the next phase of her career really did need to take place in a whole new world.

## XXII: The Final Straw

*"An entrepreneur tends to bite off a little more than he can chew, hoping he'll quickly learn how to chew it." — Roy Ash, co-founder of Litton Industries*

When I first met Diane, she was frustrated and unhappy woman. Her boss, she said, undervalued her. She knew she had brought hundreds of thousands of dollars' worth of value to the business in the form of new client relationships, probably more. She was, she insisted, the economic and creative engine that drove small PR agency for which she worked. And yet she was making exactly the same salary she had when she first began.

The inequity of this state of affairs had been bothering her for months. The deep sense of unfairness in her working situation, in fact, was the reason she had reached out to me in the first place. Would I help her figure out how to get the compensation she deserved?

Diane was a realist. She understood, all too well by now, that working for a small business, one that had been launched

16-28: Unleash the Passions of Your Youth…

recently by an entrepreneur or founder, typically meant making sacrifices — at least in the early going. But Diane had been working for her boss Milt for over two years, and she now felt she had been making sacrifices for more than long enough. The business was not struggling. To the contrary, it appeared to be thriving. Every time she raised the issue or her compensation with Milt, he told her that the topic was not "ripe for discussion" yet.

"'Ripe for discussion'?" she said indignantly during our first session. "What does that mean?"

I had no good answer.

Diane was uncomfortable not controlling her own world. She was in her mid-thirties, had ample experience in her field, and knew both what she was good at and what she wasn't. She was also quite clear on what she felt needed to happen next. She wanted one of two things to happen: a new compensation plan, based on the actual dollar value of the clients she brought into the business; or a new position someplace else. In either case, she wanted to call her own shots.

Of course, I was curious to get all the details of Diane's situation. But my first thought, the thought that crosses my mind when dealing with many entrepreneurs in waiting, was that this seemed like the kind of restless, results-driven, energetic person who ought to be running her own business.

## XXIII: If You Can't Find an Opening, Make One

*"Trust your instinct to the end, though you can render no reason." — Ralph Waldo Emerson*

16-28: Unleash the Passions of Your Youth…

A brief discussion about her work history confirmed Diane's initial diagnosis of the situation. As far as I could tell, there was unlikely to be any major lateral move, any undiscovered golden opportunity, at her current place of employment. If she was going to move forward there, she was going to have to transform her formal compensation package and her relationship with Milt, and given what I was hearing, that didn't seem likely in the near future. The PR outfit where she worked had been a one-man shop for several years, and although there were now half-a-dozen employees, it was still, in essence, a one-man shop. Milt ran a tight ship, and he expected a great deal from his small band of employees. But, from all I had been able to gather, he had not yet reached the phase in his company's development where he was willing to commit significant amounts of time, energy, attention, or capital into answering the question, "Where am I going in my career" for anyone other than himself.

This is a common pattern among entrepreneurs who are just getting their businesses off the ground. I mentioned that to Diane. Her response, an emotional one, I thought, was that, considering how hard she was working, she might as well be running the business herself!

"Have you ever considered that?" I asked.

"Considered what?" she said.

"Starting your own PR firm," I said.

She looked at me as if I were mad.

"This is about either fixing this job, or finding a new one," she pronounced, with some insistence. "That's what everyone in my family is telling me, it's what my coworkers are telling me, and

16-28: Unleash the Passions of Your Youth…

55

it's what my boyfriend is telling me. So that's what I want to focus on."

"Well, I can understand that," I said, "and I certainly do respect your opinion. But is that really what your gut is telling you?"

She had no immediate response to that.

## XXIV: The Unknown

*"Let us step into the night and pursue that flighty temptress, Adventure."—J. K. Rowling*

"It doesn't really matter what my gut is telling me," Diane said, finally. "I'm just not ready to be an entrepreneur."

"Why do you say that?" I asked.

"For the same reason I choose to rent instead of buying a home," she said. "When something goes wrong, when there's a crack in the ceiling or a leak in the plumbing, I want it to be someone else's responsibility to fix that. There's too much responsibility."

"You know," I said, "the best entrepreneurs do learn to delegate. Ultimately, of course, the owner of the company is the person who's accountable... but I've never yet met a truly successful entrepreneur who wasn't good at making sure the members of the supporting cast took on the responsibilities he or she couldn't handle. In fact, that's pretty much the job description. Doing what you're best at, and then finding ways to get others to fill in the blanks. That's really the growth cycle of a good startup."

She thought about this for a moment, but was still skeptical.

16-28: Unleash the Passions of Your Youth...

"Too much uncertainty. Too much drama. Too many unknowns. Too many blind alleys. What would happen if I ran out of money? What would happen if I had lost a big customer? What would happen if the economy went south? How would I prepare for that?"

"Those," I said, "are exactly the kinds of question entrepreneurs ask. I'm impressed!"

She looked at me curiously.

The discussion continued along these lines, which was part of what was so intriguing to me. On and on she went, patiently cataloguing the many reasons why it made absolutely no sense for her to start business of her own. The subject did not change. The very fact that she given it this much thought, and was discussing it with such animation, suggested to me that entrepreneurship was, at the very least a possibility worth exploring a little further. I explained as much to Diane, and also explained my experience with clients who had walked in the door certain that they were not "cut out" to be entrepreneurs, and had then concluded that, contrary to their own initial expectations, that was exactly what they turned out to be cut out for. At the very least, their experiences suggested that it was worth looking with curiosity towards the unknown, in awareness of the possibility that it might connect with something important in the known.

She heard me out and eventually decided to keep an open mind on the subject of entrepreneurship.

So it was that we set out to do an analysis of Diane's personal history and in particular her 16 - 28 history. What had it prepared her for?

16-28: Unleash the Passions of Your Youth…

## XXV: The Passion

What, I asked Diane, had been her chief passion in college?

This was the first of a planned ten or twelve questions I had
meant to ask her that day about her 16 - 28 experiences ... but it
was, it turned out, the most important question of all. It occupied
us for more than an hour. And Diane, I soon learned, had had no
problem answering it whatsoever.

She knew exactly what her driving passion had been during her
college years, and she loved talking about it. She had been hip
deep in putting out the college newspaper, from her freshman
year right through her senior year. That newspaper had almost
been a second major, and was certainly the target of most her
productive working hours, exceeding even the time she spent on
classwork.

What aspects of running the newspaper, I asked innocently, had
she been involved in?

The answer, I soon learned, was everything.

She had written Op-Ed pieces. She had written news stories. She
had written a monthly gossip column. She had written
interviews, and had secured face time with major celebrities,
such as an Oscar-winning actress, as part of that assignment.

But her commitment had not stopped there. She had sold
advertisements. She had laid the papers out, learning the
University's computerized typesetting system more or less
overnight when the student responsible for layout had called in
sick. She had proofread everything. She had even, at one point,
delivered the papers to their 15 on-campus distribution points,

16-28: Unleash the Passions of Your Youth...

58

when a strike threatened to prevent school-wide visibility of an important story that she had written.

"Hmm…" I said after listening to this torrent for about 45 minutes. "I can't help but notice that you're quite engaged emotionally when you speak about this. Your body language changes. You lean forward in your chair. You seem committed to getting the paper out.

"I guess that's true," Diane said. "I really do love remembering that part of my life. I loved putting out that paper. And, I have to tell you the truth here; I missed the paper quite a bit once I graduated."

"If you think about it," I said, "doing what you did for four years at that college newspaper was, eventually, a little bit like running your own business. By the end of the four years, weren't you at the center of pretty much everything?"

"Yes," Diane answered thoughtfully. "Yes, I guess I was."

## XXVI: The Possibility

*"Man often becomes what he believes himself to be. If I keep on saying to myself that I cannot do a certain thing, it is possible that I may end by really becoming incapable of doing it. On the contrary, if I have the belief that I can do it, I shall surely acquire the capacity to do it even if I may not have it at the beginning." — Mahatma Gandhi*


"So," I asked, "if you were going to open your own business, what kind of business would it be?"


16-28: Unleash the Passions of Your Youth…

"A PR agency, of course," she said. The answer came so easily and so naturally that is was hard for me to believe she hadn't given the issue some kind of thought prior to this discussion.

"Focusing on what kinds of clients?"

Diane thought about that for moment and then said, "Well, I would probably focus on successful young entrepreneurs as my target market, the ones who have the greatest potential for growth in the relationship, the greatest potential to benefit, from good PR because they want to scale up their businesses, and the greatest ease of placement. They can be business stories, human interest stories, and because they're so well networked, they can drive social media traffic like crazy. This is a group that I've been trying to get Milt to focus on more, and so far Milt hasn't seen fit to pay any attention to it."

"That's interesting," I said. "What do you think would be some of the best ways for you to distinguish yourself from your potential competitors?"

"Well," she said, "that would be an ongoing issue, but I guess I would have to make sure that I launched an agency that had an extremely strong social media presence, since the market that I'm targeting would definitely be hooked in to interactive media. I guess that would be the starting point. To establish a real foothold with entrepreneurs who are trying to establish and sustain communities in places like Google+ and Facebook and Twitter."

"Would you face any logistical difficulties in starting your own business?" I asked. "If you were to decide to go that route, I mean. Did you sign anything?"

16-28: Unleash the Passions of Your Youth...

60

"No. There was no non-compete agreement or anything like that. That's pretty much unenforceable in our industry."

"Have you talked this over with him?" I asked.

"A dozen times, maybe more. He always tells me to feel free to move on if I'm not happy with the way things are going. I think he's kind of daring me to quit. And betting I won't."

"So why don't you?"

She thought about that for a while, and finally said, "Fear."

"Fear of what?" I asked.

"Fear of not measuring up. Fear of the unknown. Fear of not being able to find clients, I guess."

"Can I ask you a question?"

"Sure."

"What are you doing for a living right now? Finding clients, right?"

She smiled and nodded.

"So here's the downside. What happens if you don't do anything? What happens if you just stay with what's familiar from here on out? Is there anything scary about that?"

Diane said she'd sleep on it. There was a lot to think about.

## XXVII: The Bicycle Rider

*"After a thousand years pass, it builds its own funeral pyre, lining it with cinnamon, myrrh and cassia. Climbing to a rest on the very top, it examines the world all throughout*
16-28: Unleash the Passions of Your Youth...

*the night with the ability to see true good and evil. When the sun rises the next morning, with great sorrow for all that it sees, it sings a haunting song. As it sings, the heat of the sun ignites the expensive spices and the Phoenix dies in the flames. But the Phoenix is not remarkable for its feathers or flames. It is most revered for its ability to climb from its own funeral pyre, from the very ashes of its old charred body, as a brand new life ready to live again once more. Life after life, it goes through this cycle. It absorbs human sorrow, only to rise from death to do it all again. It never wearies, it never tires. It never questions its fate. Some say that the Phoenix is real, that it exists somewhere out there in the mountains of Arabia, elusive and mysterious. Others say that the Phoenix is only a wish made by desperate humans to believe in the continuance of life. But I know a secret. We are the Phoenix." — Courtney Cole,* Every Last Kiss

It was as though Diane had learned to fly overnight.

In our final coaching session, I noticed immediately that she was standing more erect, sitting in her chair straighter, engaging me with greater confidence, and making more eye contact. She seemed happier, more satisfied with her own choices, and far less likely to end her sentences in mid phrase than she had been the first few times we met.

She had, I realized quickly, rediscovered herself.

It almost came as no surprise to learn that she had decided that doing nothing was a lot scarier than starting her own company.

"You were absolutely right," she said. "It's just like being back in the newsroom of the college paper. That seemed scary at first, too. But back in college, I asked myself the same kind of

16-28: Unleash the Passions of Your Youth…

question. How would I feel if four years went by without at least trying for the editor's spot. So I went for it, Once I began thinking of it that way, about how much I'd regret it if I didn't at least give this a shot, at least try launching my own company, everything began falling into place. The planning, the negotiating, the interviewing. I can see how it will all come together again. It's like picking up a bicycle I hadn't ridden in a long time and remembering that I knew how to pedal."

She was back on the bike, peddling with vigor and energy. And she now knew exactly where she was going.

## XXVIII: A Happy Ending Is Only the Beginning

When I last saw Diane, it was at a convention. She was working the aisles, talking up her business, and as comfortable an entrepreneur as I had ever seen. I was taken aback by how confident and poised she seemed, and by what a stark contrast she presented to the timid, tentative figure who had been so fixated on what she could not do and how her employer had mistreated her. Now, two years later, she had successfully launched her PR company, and was widely regarded as an expert in her field, and her company now employed seven people. She was working with major clients in film, television, and the business world. She was on her game.

Diane had not only found her true calling. She had found her true self. This really was the person that she was meant to be. As I watched her interact with people, I thought that, while it was certainly true that not everyone is cut out to be an entrepreneur, it's also true that some people really are. Diane was one of those who were born to run her own business, and I was honored to have helped her come to that realization.

16-28: Unleash the Passions of Your Youth…

Over lunch, I asked her whether she would do anything differently, if she had it all to do over again. Without a moment's hesitation, she told me: "Yes, I do have a regret. I wish I had started the process with you earlier. I wish we had talked about the school paper and what I learned there two years before we did. I wish I had woken up then, when I first started feeling restless in my old job. I would've gotten a better sense of where I was supposed to go. I could've saved several years, gotten the company off the launching pad earlier, and had a lot more fun.

"I should've realized long before I did that what I really needed to do was to put myself back in the middle of things, calling the shots. It's where I belong, and it took me longer to figure that out then it probably should have. But at least I figured it out!"

And with that, she finished her lunch, thanked me again, and made her way back to her company's booth. She was on duty.

16-28: Unleash the Passions of Your Youth…

## Case IV: Pacing Yourself
## Youth ... and Emerging Adulthood Lesson Four: Know When a Long-Term Plan Makes the Most Sense
### XXIX: Moving On

*"You can't stop the future; you can't rewind the past; the only way to learn the secret ... is to press Play."*—Jay Asher

My next client, Walt, approached me after he had he had heard me speak at a local business gathering.

He made his way through the group that always gathers after a good speech, waited his turn patiently, shook my hand, and introduced himself. He had recently relocated to Fairfield. Would I be willing to talk through some career issues that he was trying to sort out? I told him I would, and we set our first meeting for the following week.

Some people are hesitant about sharing their most important 16-28 experiences with me, but Walt was not one of those. He brought a fascinating personal history to our first session. A decade or so earlier, he had been a hot prospect for the major leagues as a baseball pitcher. Having dominated his sport in college, and having played a single, very strong season in the minor leagues, he made his way onto the list of "left-handers to watch" for a shot at the big leagues.

Of course, reaching that point in his sports career meant creating a level of discipline, commitment, and sacrifice in his life that most people never experience. His family, I learned, had shared

16-28: Unleash the Passions of Your Youth...

65

in all those sacrifices, and supported him fully. Once he committed to his goal everyone in his circle was eager to help him fulfill his dream of becoming a successful major league pitcher.

But then, in the season before his predicted debut at the triple A level, which is the level right below the big leagues, Walt blew out his shoulder, and his baseball career was over.

It's odd how things work out in life. For some people, a setback but like that would have been something close to a traumatic experience; in fact, Walt's story initially reminded me of other former athletes I knew, like Bobby Valentine, who had been shaken to the core by career-ending injuries.

But Walt was a different kind of guy. He was not there to talk to me about his transition out of the world of sports. He'd already made that transition. He was there to talk to me about a very different type of career change.

Shortly after learning that he was no longer a major league prospect, Walt did his own self-assessment and decided that he would build a career based on his passion for numbers and statistics. His transition was a careful, well-conceived one, and it drew on his strengths. Throughout his college and minor-league career, Walt had been the guy on the bench keeping track of the balls and strikes, totaling up the earned-run averages, and, after the game, analyzing which pitchers, including himself, fell behind on the count and why.

He really had an amazing head for figures, and, as he told me, his decision to move from the world of sports into the world of mortgage underwriting was a natural and successful one. I could tell he was an ambitious, committed guy who was likely to succeed in whatever field he chose to pursue.

16-28: Unleash the Passions of Your Youth…

In fact, Walt had worked his way up quite quickly from an entry-level position as a senior underwriting executive at a major Midwestern bank. It had taken him less than 10 years. He had been pulling down a six-figure income ... until recently.

About a year before Walt and I had met, everything had changed. Walt's wife Jean, who had put her own career on hold after the birth of their daughter, decided when their little girl turned two, it would be time to re-enter the job market. Like Walt, she was a bit of an overachiever, and she was eager to get back on track. She learned of a job opening in Connecticut, where I live, and she pursued it with all the energy, commitment, and persistence that had distinguished the first phase of her career is the insurance industry. She got a very lucrative job offer from one of the top food companies in the country, and the second phase of her career had begun.

Walt agreed to move from the Midwest, where all his contacts and all of his experience in business were, so that he could support his wife by enabling her to pursue her own career. He put his own career on hold, resigned, moved to Connecticut with his young family, and spent a year as the primary caregiver for their daughter.

The reason he wanted to talk to me was simple. He had spent a "wonderful" year helping to raise their daughter, and he had no bad feelings at all about doing that while his wife re-established herself. But now his daughter was old enough to go to daycare, and Walt wanted my help in figuring out exactly what he should do next, and how he should go about doing it.

He thought he wanted to start his own company.

Did I think that was a good idea?

16-28: Unleash the Passions of Your Youth...

## XXX: What's Next?

*"I may not have gone where I intended to go, but I think I have ended up where I needed to be."* — *Douglas Adams,* The Long Dark Tea-Time of the Soul

Was it a good idea for Walt to start this kind of company? You run into a lot of questions like that in my line of work.

I did not answer Walt's query immediately. I knew I didn't have enough information to even begin to answer it. Ultimately, of course, it was not my job to decide whether that kind of entrepreneurial leap was a good idea, but rather Walt's job ... although I certainly had an obligation to share my opinion on the matter during our sessions. My first thought, the one that raced into my brain before I had even summoned it, was that "starting a company" can mean very different things to different people.

To someone like Diane, "starting a company" had meant leveraging a clear set of skills and experiences in service of a (long-dormant, but still quite strong) aptitude for risk-taking and entrepreneurship. It had also meant taking a clear, no-nonsense look at exactly what Diane's background and personal inventory told her about what she should and shouldn't be doing next with her life. And finally, it had meant conducting a sober analysis of both the industry and the market she hoped to enter, so that we could create a viable list of possible next steps for her to consider pursuing. In her case, that last part -- the sober analysis of the industry and the market — had shown a spotlight on a wide-open market terrain, a vast universe of prospects, no single dominant player, and few meaningful barriers to entry. Starting a small PR firm, and growing it over time, made perfect sense for Diane. In

16-28: Unleash the Passions of Your Youth…

her case, making the transition into entrepreneurship had been not just a good idea, but a great idea.

Walt, however, still presented only question marks to me. Well — that wasn't quite accurate. I did know that the type of company he wanted to start, and the companies he wanted to compete against, handled tens of millions of dollars of transactions, were heavily regulated, and typically employed scores or even hundreds of employees. Even if all the stars aligned for him, this was not going to be an overnight startup.

I told Walt that neither of us had enough information yet to answer his question ... and that, ultimately, it would be his question to answer.

"In order for either of us to get to the point where we have any sense of whether or not this makes sense for you," I said, "my experience is that we need to do three things. First, we need to look at the most important formative experiences in your life, whether or not you think they relate to the business you are considering starting. Typically, these are experiences that happened to you between the ages of sixteen and twenty-eight. Second, we need to do an assessment of your most important workplace contributions, so we can identify the places where you feel most comfortable adding value. And third, we want to find the best options for you moving forward. One of those might be launching a company -- or it might not. We really don't know yet. I will say that's a pretty complex field that you're thinking of launching into."

Walt laughed. He knew that, he said, and he understood and respected my process. What I had outlined for him sounded like exactly what he wanted to do next.

He asked me how we should get started.

16-28: Unleash the Passions of Your Youth…

"Well," I said, "given your background, I'm kind of curious about how you got into minor-league baseball."

"Sure," he said -- but I could tell from the tone of his voice and from his body language that his was a little hesitant to begin with this topic.

"What's the matter?" I asked. "You sound like that's not how you had imagined our session beginning."

"Well, I guess it isn't."

"Why not?"

"Do you want to take a guess at how many people ask me to talk about how I got into minor league baseball in an average week?"

I smiled. "Okay. Well, what *do* you want to talk about?"

He seemed relieved.

"Did you say," he asked a little tentatively, "that we could talk about the most important formative experience that ever happened to me, whether or not it connected to the kind of company I want to start?"

"Absolutely," I said. "That's one of the very best ways to get started."

"And it can be something that happened to me between the ages of sixteen and twenty-eight?"

"That's where the most important experiences usually wait to be rediscovered," I said.

"Well, I know exactly what it is," he said, grinning wide.

16-28: Unleash the Passions of Your Youth…

"What?" I asked.

"It's not what happened to me on the way into baseball," Walt said. "It's what happened to me on the way out of it."

## XXXI: Crisis or Opportunity

*"You may encounter many defeats, but you must not be defeated. In fact, it may be necessary to encounter the defeats, so you can know who you are, what you can rise from, how you can still come out of it." — Maya Angelou*

I asked Walt what he meant. Without missing a beat, he told me that his torn rotator cuff, the injury that had ended his professional baseball career, was the single best thing that had ever happened to him.

"That's interesting," I said. "Most people who go through anything similar to what you went through don't see it that way." And I briefly referenced Juan's story, explaining how the end of his athletic career had been a kind of personal and professional crisis.

"Well I didn't feel like I was going through a crisis," Walt said. "In fact, when I figured out that I wasn't going to be able to pitch professionally anymore, the first thing I felt was relief."

"Relief? Really?"

"Absolutely," he said.

"How's that?" I asked.

"Because up until that point," he explained, "I was basically being an athlete not just for myself, but for myself and for

16-28: Unleash the Passions of Your Youth…

71

everyone else in my family. Finally, I was making my own choices."

"Interesting."

"Don't get me wrong," he went on, "I really loved playing baseball, and I really loved being good at it. I knew I had the chance to have a good career in the game. I knew I had a shot at making the big leagues. And as long as all that was in play, I was more than happy to work as hard at baseball as I possibly could. I am proud that I was as single-minded about baseball as I did. I fought for it as hard as I could. But I knew that, no matter how much promise I had, the odds were long against me making the big leagues — just because the odds are long against ANYONE making the big leagues, no matter how good they were.

"So when I got cut, and when I found out my fastball was never going to go above 75 miles an hour, no matter how great a recovery I made, I felt a relief. Why? Because then I could look all the family members who had supported me for so many years and tell them, honestly, with a straight face, that I had given this my best shot. And that it hadn't worked out."

He smiled.

"But in my heart," he said, "I was nothing but relieved. This meant I could finally start building exactly what I wanted to build with my life. I knew I wasn't going to be an athlete my whole life. And I could start moving on to that chapter on my own terms. I saw all this as an opportunity, not as a closed door. And that wasn't double-talk. It was how I really felt."

"Interesting," I said. "So if it wasn't what happened on the mound, what DID you use to help you decide what you wanted to focus on next in your career?"

16-28: Unleash the Passions of Your Youth…

He smiled at me.

"My time in the dugout."

## XXXII: The Dugout

*"We do not need magic to transform our world. We carry all of the power we need inside ourselves already."* — *J.K. Rowling*

"About a month or so after I got out of baseball," Walt said, "a friend of mine and I went out to a local pub for a beer. He had just broken up with his girlfriend. I don't remember whether he was trying to cheer me up, or I was trying to cheer him up, but I'm pretty sure someone was trying to cheer someone up. Along about the third Sam Adams, he asked me how I would describe what had just happened to me, and I said, 'It was a horrible breakthrough.'"

"He looked at me kind of funny, then asked me to explain exactly what I meant by each of those words. I remember I had done a lot of thinking about this, thanks to a long talk with my own girlfriend — the woman I later married."

"I told my buddy what she'd told me — that getting cut was horrible, but it wasn't JUST horrible. Because I knew I didn't want to spend my whole life in baseball, and I couldn't have put any more into the game than I had. I knew I'd given it my level best, and I knew I had nothing to be ashamed of. Yes, there was time to be disappointed, but when that part was done — my girlfriend had told me — then there would be time for a breakthrough, too. So: A horrible breakthrough."

16-28: Unleash the Passions of Your Youth…

"Well, my buddy was pretty impressed by that. He smiled, toasted me and my girlfriend, took a long pull off of his own beer, and then asked me what my breakthrough was going to be."

"And then I had to look him in the eye and tell him I had no idea."

"He laughed pretty loud about that, and then did me the biggest favor that anyone has done before or since. He asked me a great question. He looked me straight in the eye and said, 'Well, if you DID know what your breakthrough looked like, what would you see yourself doing as a result?' "

"That one really spun my head around, and I don't think it was just the music and the lights and the beer. If I could see myself AFTER the next big breakthrough in my life ... what would I be doing? It had to be something that I loved. I knew that much. I knew I wouldn't be pitching, but that wasn't the only thing I had loved doing in my life. What ELSE had I loved doing? When I WASN'T pitching?"

"I only had to think for a moment, and then I saw myself doing it. I was sitting in the dugout finding patterns in data, in numbers. And suddenly it made perfect sense. I realized that the thing I had loved doing most, even more than pitching, was sitting in the dugout tracking pitches, then feeding the data into a spreadsheet so the manager and the pitching coach could make sense of it all. So I could make sense of it all. I loved doing that."

"What kind of pitch had each pitcher thrown? A slider? A fastball? A curve? A change-up? A screwball? What had the count been when he threw it? What had happened as a result of that pitch being thrown? Was the batter right- or left-handed?

16-28: Unleash the Passions of Your Youth...

What pitch worked best against what batter, in what situation? What pitch had worked worst?"

"At that moment, sitting there in the bar with my buddy, I realized that it hadn't just been baseball that I had loved. It had been numbers, too. I was great with numbers. In fact, I had been so good with them that I was the guy the manager always wanted in the dugout tracking pitches. When I wasn't pitching, I was crunching numbers. I looked at my buddy, and I smiled, and I said, 'I've got it. I've got my breakthrough."

"He said, 'Yeah? What is it?'"

"And I said, "All I've got to do is get back in the dugout and track pitches ... without actually going back in the dugout to track pitches."

"He didn't know what the hell I was talking about ... but I did. And that's what mattered."

## XXXIII: Integrity

*"**Be Impeccable With Your Word**. Speak with integrity. Say only what you mean. Avoid using the word to speak against yourself or to gossip about others. Use the power of your word in the direction of truth and love. **Don't Take Anything Personally**. Nothing others do is because of you. What others say and do is a projection of their own reality, their own dream. When you are immune to the opinions and actions of others, you won't be the victim of needless suffering. **Don't Make Assumptions.** Find the courage to ask questions and to express what you really want. Communicate with others as clearly as you can to avoid misunderstandings, sadness and drama. With just this one agreement, you can completely transform your life. **Always Do Your Best.** Your best is going to change from moment*

16-28: Unleash the Passions of Your Youth…

75

*to moment; it will be different when you are healthy as opposed to sick. Under any circumstance, simply do your best, and you will avoid self-judgment, self-abuse and regret." — Miguel Ruiz*

From that point forward, Walt and his wife Jean were focused on integrity in their working lives. In the early years of his marriage, he had definitely taken the lead in terms of establishing a solid career track for himself that was rooted in integrity.

Let me explain what I mean by that. Walt had been given the discernment, the wisdom, the insight, and the maturity necessary to take what had happened to him in the world of professional baseball as a beginning, and not as an end. He had a healthy sense of self, one that was not based on his achievements on the field, but rather on whether he had given his best effort. Secure in the knowledge that he really had made his best effort in his pitching career, he was okay with where that career had led him. Having reached the point where he had played one game with integrity, he was ready to enter another. And he knew he would have to draw on the skills he had developed on the bench in order to do that

"The game I left behind was one I had played with an outstanding support network," he told me. "Remember, I was still very young. I was only twenty when I blew my shoulder out, and just about everything I had done in my career had been done with a crowd of supporting, positive people around me. There was my family, which was a big one. There was always family at all my junior high and high school games, and there was usually family at my home games when I was pitching in the pros, because the team I pitched for happened to be within an hour's

16-28: Unleash the Passions of Your Youth…

drive of my family's home. There were coaches and managers — dozens of them — and there were lots of scouts and front-office people. There was my agent. I had a lot of people rooting for me when I was out there on the mound every five days, and I had a lot of people rooting for me in the off-season."

"But once I decided with certainty that I was going to build my next career around numbers, once I made up my mind that I was going to get my degree in accounting and then move into banking, I was on my own."

"There was something a little scary about that ... but there was also something exciting about it. It was kind of like I had made my declaration of independence. I was building a new place for myself and for Jean, and I was doing it on my own. Not with a tribe of relatives and an army of coaches. Just Jean and me. That motivated me."

"Nobody believes me when I say this, but having to set out on my own after baseball was over was a completely liberating experience for me. It let me shine a spotlight on a part of myself that wasn't based on everyone's expectations about how I would or wouldn't perform on the mound on any given day. I was able to build a new space for myself that was connected to something I loved just as much as baseball — numbers and analysis — and I was doing it all on my own. It felt great. It was exactly where I was supposed to be going in my life. I just had this feeling — and my wife Jean had it, too — that as long as I maintained integrity with that new Walt, the one I was building when I enrolled in college and started studying accounting, everything was going to come out just fine."

"And it did."

## XXXIV: The Right Next Step
16-28: Unleash the Passions of Your Youth…

*"Far better it is to dare mighty things, to win glorious triumphs, even though checkered by failure, than to take rank with those poor spirits who neither enjoy much nor suffer much because they live in the gray twilight that knows neither victory nor defeat."– Theodore Roosevelt*

Walt was one of those rare clients who already had a clear and generally accurate idea of where he added value and how he wanted to add it. The question before us now was one of scale:

Should he "follow his dream" and begin the arduous task of launching a mortgage banking enterprise? Or should he pursue a more traditional career path, and "settle" for a salaried position similar to the one he had left behind, back when he had agreed to stay home and support his family's home life?

These were the two possible "next steps" Walt had identified, the two options that he saw on his radar screen during our early discussions. He was inclining toward the latter course, but he wanted some guidance and some insight so that he could be certain that he was making the right decision for both himself and his family. I should emphasize here that Walt was an extremely goal-oriented individual, and that he loved big, energizing, goals. The goal of making it to the major leagues had been replaced in his life, more or less seamlessly, by the goal of creating a stable, loving home environment during his daughter's first two years of life. Now that that had been accomplished, he was eager to choose the next big, fat, exciting goal.

His heart (he told me) was telling him that he could and should run his own company, that he was ready for that step.

16-28: Unleash the Passions of Your Youth…

His head, however, was wary of the many obstacles to successful entrepreneurship in the field he had chosen. This was not like starting a software firm or a design company, after all. Launching a new operation of the kind he was envisioning would require major alliance he did not yet have, substantial assets that were not at his disposal, and significant human resources, not the least of which was someone with the capacity to clear daunting regulatory hurdles.

"So which is right?" he asked me at one point. "My head or my heart? Which do I follow?" I think he expected me to tell him that he should shelve his dream and pursue a traditional career track.

He looked more than a little shocked when I told him he should follow both his head *and* his heart.

What I meant by that was that, for Walt, entrepreneurship was likely to require more allies, more patience, and more preparation than it was for someone operating in a different industry. So his head was right when he said that he should pursue a more traditional career path right now — because that career path could direct him toward the resources and the contacts he would need down the road. But his heart was right when it told him that he should take clear steps toward his ultimate goal of launching a mortgage banking operation.

He really could do both. There was no need to choose between the two. All we had to do was create a good long-term plan together, the kind of plan that had a realistic likelihood of getting him exactly where he wanted to go within the next three to five years. I asked Walt whether he was willing to work with me to create that kind of plan, and his eyes lit up.

"You know what this is going to be like?" he said, smiling.

16-28: Unleash the Passions of Your Youth…

"No, what?" I asked.

"The plan I built for myself for getting from college into the major leagues. I couldn't do that overnight, either. I had to take it step by step, just like I'll be taking it here. But the difference now is, I've got a much better shot of actually attaining my goal within the time-frame of the plan!"

I agreed. "You're still going where you're supposed to go," I said. "You're just going to be taking a different route."

"I'm going to be taking the right route," he said. "The route that's based on getting exactly where I want to go, exactly how I want to get there."

## XXXV: The Five-Year Plan

*"Water does not resist. Water flows. When you plunge your hand into it, all you feel is a caress. Water is not a solid wall, it will not stop you. But water always goes where it wants to go, and nothing in the end can stand against it. Water is patient. Dripping water wears away a stone. Remember that, my child. Remember you are half water. If you can't go through an obstacle, go around it. Water does."* — *Margaret Atwood,* The Penelopiad

The path forward that Walt and I put together was one that kept as many options as possible for him, both in the short and the long term. The short-term goal was to re-enter the job market in a way that did justice to his significant experience, background, and accomplishments; the long term goal was to get him to a point where he would be in a good position to launch his own operation within the next five years.

16-28: Unleash the Passions of Your Youth…

He had come from a salary level where it was realistic for him to expect to invest between four and six months to find the right full-time job if he was working on his own and focusing full-time on trying to set up interviews. We decided to try to accelerate that process by pointing Walt toward appropriate freelance opportunities within three areas that supported his near-term aspirations as well as his longer-term ones: commercial real estate, banking, and financial services. I also made a point of introducing him to a number of key people at companies and recruiting organizations; one in particular was a former client in the commercial real estate business I had worked with before on multiple occasions.

It turned out to be a good mix. Walt was able to sign on for some lucrative real estate project work within just sixty days, and that series of projects eventually led to substantial opportunities elsewhere. Walt was broadening the level of experience on his resume — and just as important, he was expanding his contact network here in Connecticut, which was, after all, where he wanted to work now. It took just a little over ninety days for him to secure the kind of position he wanted. I would like to think that all of that was attributable to the plan he and I created, but the truth of the matter is that he is the one who executed the plan.

One evening at dinner with his family, I asked Walt's wife whether she was surprised at how quickly Walt had been able to settle himself into a new career track in Connecticut. "Not really," she said, smiling. "He tends to get what he wants once he figures out what it is."

Walt is now a full-time real estate underwriter and analyst. He's working for a major national bank with offices in Connecticut. His five-year plan is on track. He is doing what he loves, a step

16-28: Unleash the Passions of Your Youth...

81

at a time … he is getting closer every day to launching the company of his dreams … and he is doing all of it his way.

## Case V: Moving On
## Youth ... and Emerging Adulthood Lesson Five: Graduate from Relationships That Are Holding You Back
### XXXVI: Family Matters

*"All happy families are alike; each unhappy family is unhappy in its own way."* — *Leo Tolstoy,* Anna Karenina

One of the most powerful examples of the transformative power of the career diagnostic process I have called the 16 - 28 Solution came my way about five years ago.

The client's name was Sam. He was the owner-operator of a home improvement company that has been in business in our area for years — decades, even. I remembered passing the building He had reached out to me by phone; a former client of mine had referred him to me. He said his issue was urgent, that he had heard good things about my services, and that he was curious about whether it would be possible for us to meet immediately — tomorrow, say.

Curious, I said, "My day tomorrow is booked, but if the issue is urgent, I can move an appointment around and see you at ten o'clock. Just out of curiosity, could I ask whether you happen to work for Superior Home Improvement?"

"That's right," Sam said.

"Would that by any chance happen to be a family-owned business?"

"It would. How did you know?"

16-28: Unleash the Passions of Your Youth...

83

"Let's call it a lucky guess for now. I'll see you tomorrow."

In fact, it had been anything but a lucky guess. There is a certain tone that creeps into a prospective client's voice, particularly during the very first telephone conversation, that I have come to associate with problems that connect to a family business. The tone is not exactly one of desperation, but instead one of intense purpose. It is not a tone of WANTING to resolve a problem related to one's work as of NEEDING to resolve it, of not being able to put up with the status quo for a day or a minute longer. This insistent, tone of voice is peculiar, I have noticed, to clients who have both a business and a complex series of family relationships at stake.

These clients are always interesting, because the usually find themselves in quite difficult situations that present personal, familial, and professional challenges, all at the same time. The challenges are unique to both the individual and the family. You never heard the same story twice with these clients … but the stories always revolved around a critical 16 - 28 incident.

I rescheduled my ten o'clock appointment … and wondered what Sam would bring to the table.

## XXXVII: The Problem Employee

*"It's not denial. I'm just selective about the reality I accept."* — Bill Watterson

As first conversations very often did, my initial discussion with Sam involved a subject that seemed like the cause. It was actually a symptom.

16-28: Unleash the Passions of Your Youth…

84

Sam was convinced that the real problem was simple and clear-cut. He explained that all he needed was my recommendation on how best to solve it. He described it in simple terms. He had a veteran employee named Bill who was letting both Sam and the company down, and who needed to shape up. My job was to give him the answer to the question, "How do I motivate Bill?"

It seemed a little early for that. I suggested that many problems— in business and in larger life — are interrelated. I also suggested that identifying the answer to that one question might not solve the underlying problem Sam was facing.

Sam shook his head vigorously. He knew he was facing a crisis, and he knew that crises sometimes have complex causes. In this case, he insisted, he was absolutely certain the crisis had one and only one cause: Bill's unacceptable performance. The reason he was paying me for my time was simple: He wanted to identify the technique that would give him back his star performer. He didn't want to lose Bill. And he wanted me to tell him what he had to do to save him.

I bit my lip, then asked, "Well, what seems to be the problem with Bill?"

"Escalating absenteeism. A complete collapse in productivity. Terrible attitude. Total inability to manage subordinates. It's not even the same person I hired thirteen years ago. That guy was not only my best employee — he was my best friend. I want that guy back again. And you've got to help me track him down. We've got to re-motivate him."

It turned out that Sam had tried every conceivable tactic for "re-motivating" Bill, who was (or had once been) the operations manager. No matter what tactic Sam had tried, it only seemed to make Bill's performance problems worsen. He had taken him out

16-28: Unleash the Passions of Your Youth...

to lunch to talk things over; he had given Bill specific performance targets, based on in-depth, collaborative discussions; he had called members of Bill's family and attempted to enlist their help. Nothing had worked. His performance had only gotten worse.

"Well, I hate to be the one to suggest this," I said cautiously, "but the pattern you're describing sounds like it might match up with a substance abuse problem. Have you asked Bill to take a drug test?"

Sam sat up rigid in his chair and stared at me as though I had suggested treason. There was a pause.

"That's not the way we do things at our company," he said, ominously quiet. "What you're suggesting would lead to a complete failure in morale, up and down the entire team. It would send the message that management doesn't trust people to do their jobs."

## XXXVIII: The Bump in The Road

*"I do not trust people who don't love themselves and yet tell me, 'I love you.' There is an African saying which is: Be careful when a naked person offers you a shirt." —* *Maya Angelou*

I asked Sam to share a little bit about Bill's history with the company, so that I could get a better sense of how this "morale problem" had come about.

Sam said he was happy to share all the details. Sam's uncle — the founder of the company — had hired Bill years ago. He had worked his way up the ladder quickly, and was "like one of the family." (That was a telling description coming from someone
16-28: Unleash the Passions of Your Youth…

like Sam, whose whole career had played out within a single family-owned business.) For over a decade Bill had been an exemplary contributor and one of the most important company leaders. People had looked to him regularly for advice, for insights, and even for moral guidance when they were facing big problems in their lives. Last but certainly not least, Sam informed me, he knew his job inside and out. He understood inventory, ordering procedures, and assembly better than anyone else in the building. For years, Sam explained, he had been rock-solid, the most dependable guy you could ever ask for.

And then he hit a rough spot.

Something happened. Sam wasn't sure whether Bill's marriage falling apart led to the bad crowd Bill started hanging out with, or the bad crowd hastened the collapse of the marriage, but either way, it was obvious that Bill was in crisis. He had just never bounced back from that.

Had Sam ever tried to talk to Bill about what was going on in his life?

"Many times."

"What had happened?"

Bill had said he didn't want to talk about it. The meetings were always short and unproductive. He simply refused to discuss anything that connected to his problems. He felt Sam was barging into his private life, and said so.

What was behind all this, in Sam's opinion?

It was possible (Sam admitted) that Bill had a substance abuse problem. Things certainly seemed to be getting worse.

16-28: Unleash the Passions of Your Youth...

For about how long, I wondered, could that have been the case?

Sam thought for a moment, and then said, "No more than two years probably a year and a half."

That one took my breath away. A senior member of the team, at this level of dysfunction for a year and a half? No wonder the company was in trouble.

Finally, I asked: "If you had to explain, in one sentence, what had happened to Bill over the past eighteen months to someone who knew nothing about him or your company," I asked, "what would you say?"

Sam had to think about that one. Finally, he said, "He counted on us to help him get over a bump in the road after he went through that tough divorce ... and we all let him down."

## XXXIX: The Campaign

*"The measure of intelligence is the ability to change." —*
*Albert Einstein*

I wanted to look a little more closely at Sam's personal 16 - 28 experiences. Some kind of roadblock was keeping him from making a clear assessment of Bill's performance challenges. Overcoming that roadblock of Sam's, I felt, was more important than generating more information about what was and wasn't working in terms of "motivating" this problem employee.

With that in mind, I asked Sam to tell me about his early history, his teen years and his years as a young man.

A little distracted by the change in subject, Sam seemed a bit disoriented at first by the seemingly irrelevant questions I was

16-28: Unleash the Passions of Your Youth...

asking about his interests and pursuits thirty years ago. I assured him that what I was asking him about really was relevant, deeply relevant, to Bill's situation. Before long, he was following my lead, and walking me through his high school years.

One important moment during his senior year had come when he had decided to seek election as class president. Sam was popular, he was a hard worker (he was already working weekends at his uncle's store), and he was respected by most students, but his opponent was the captain of the football team -- a formidable opponent. He had started out managing the campaign with only his younger sister's help -- she had announced over dinner one night that she would serve as campaign manager -- but something went wrong. The sister, whose name was Eileen, had limited her duties to chatting up her own friends on the phone for a few minutes each day, and Sam had ended up exhausting himself in putting up posters and handing out leaflets. His own performance in class began to suffer.

Mrs. Salem, an English teacher with whom he had a good relationship, and in whose class he got straight A's, took him aside one afternoon and advised a change of strategy. Perhaps his sister had been the wrong choice as campaign manager? Another fellow — a close friend of Sam's, Chris, was well known throughout the school because of his talents as a wrestler. He was in the same English class as Sam, and to Mrs. Salem, he seemed to offer more in the way of organizational skills. Perhaps Chris would be willing to help, and Sam's sister could play a different role.

It was a brilliant idea, one that opened up all kinds of doors. Sam enlisted Mrs. Salem's help in talking to his sister, and it turned out she was fine with Chris stepping in as "co-campaign manager." Suddenly Sam had a more committed helper in

16-28: Unleash the Passions of Your Youth...

passing out flyers ... a great organizer for the campaign … and a charismatic ally in recruiting undecided voters. People were interested in what Chris had to say, and the students who were impressed by the school's sports stars now had two such stars to talk to. Within a week of Sam's talk to Mrs. Salem, the team's starting quarterback knew he had real competition.

There was to be a debate. Chris made sure that the auditorium was packed with Sam's supporters. That was the turning point of the campaign; Sam's supporters cheered more loudly and energetically than his opponent's, and Sam could feel the momentum.

The next day, he won the election. He wrote Mrs. Salem a personal thank-you note.

"Fascinating," I said.

"I guess," said Sam. "But what does it have to do with the problems I'm going through with Bill?"

"Everything," I said. "The key to resolving everything lies in what you just told me."


## XXXX: The Breakthrough

*"And the day came when the risk to remain tight in a bud was more painful than the risk it took to blossom."* — *Anaïs Nin*


Sam looked at me in complete bewilderment. "What in the world does my high-school campaign for student body president tell me about how to get Bill motivated?"

16-28: Unleash the Passions of Your Youth…

"It reframes the question. You're asking the wrong one, by the way. And I think Mrs. Salem would have been the first to tell you that."

He seemed a little taken aback to hear me say her name without permission, as though I had been rifling through his dresser drawers without permission.

"I didn't think I was asking Mrs. Salem for help here. I thought I was asking you for help."

"You are. And she's the very best coach I could find for you on this question."

"Explain, please."

"Look, Sam. Did Mrs. Salem tell you how to *motivate* Eileen?"

He thought for a moment.

"No."

"What did she do?"

"She pointed me toward someone else."

"Right."

"Yeah, but she didn't tell me to *disown* Eileen, did she? Are you saying you think I should just walk away from Bill's problems?"

"Honestly, I don't think you're getting the question right — at least not yet. It's not the way Mrs. Salem would pose it."

"Okay — I give up. What would Mrs. Salem ask?"

"You're asking me to do a role-play here?"

16-28: Unleash the Passions of Your Youth…

"Sure. So far, it's your breakthrough, not mine."

It was a fair point. I gave Sam my best Mrs. Salem impression: "Sam, can we have a word before your next class?"

"Sure, Mrs. Salem," he said with a wide smile. "What's on your mind?"

"By the way, you still owe me an essay on *Huckleberry Finn*. Anyway — it's about Bill. How long has he been working for you, now?"

"A long time."

"Mm hm. Why did you hire him?"

"Because he was damn good at what he did. Pardon the language, Mrs. Salem."

"Oh, that's no problem. Mark Twain swore, too. Look. You didn't hire him because you wanted to solve his problems for him, did you?"

"No, of course not."

"So it's a professional relationship?"

Sam paused.

"Not exclusively professional. Every employee here is family," he said finally.

"Really?"

"Really."

"So every employee gets invited to your Thanksgiving table?"

16-28: Unleash the Passions of Your Youth…

He thought about that one for a moment.

"How many employees have you got that you aren't related to by blood, Sam?"

He pondered this before answering. "About 12."

"And how many of those people do you sit down with at Thanksgiving time?"

"Um … none."

"So it's a professional relationship, right?"

"Look, I think I see where you're going with this, but you have to take a moment to understand just what kind of company we've built. We want everyone to feel LIKE they're part of the family. That's what we're all about. We don't walk out on people when they need us. Mrs. Salem."

"What makes you think you'd be walking out on him by letting him go? Look, Sam — this kind of challenge hits a lot of family businesses. How you respond to it is going to determine where you go and where your company goes. I can tell family is important to you. Of course, family can be great sometimes in real life, and it even makes a good metaphor in the workplace now and then. But there comes a point where you have to look at whether or not the professional relationship is working for either person in the relationship. Right now, it looks to me like it isn't. And here's why I say that. From your side, this problem with Bill has consumed far too much of your energy and attention for over a year and a half. And from Bill's side, there is an uncomfortable reality to confront: He's sinking deeper and deeper, and whatever you're doing about it isn't turning that cycle around. In fact, what you're doing seems to be accelerating

16-28: Unleash the Passions of Your Youth…

93

his downward spiral. How much longer do you want to do that? He's NOT family, Sam, and even if he were, he would be in more danger by staying where he is, with you helping to perpetuate this cycle. What if you thought of it this way: You're going to help him move into another situation that will be better for both of you … you're going to refocus … and you're going to bring in another campaign manager."

He stared at me for a while, and then said: "Mrs. Salem, you make some very good points. I think I need to schedule a meeting with Bill."

He pulled out his cell phone and scheduled that meeting, right there, on the spot. I saw him do it. I heard him tell Bill that it was time for a meeting of the minds. I heard him tell Bill they both needed to move on in life, and that he wanted an hour of Bill's time, face-to-face, to map out what that forward motion was going to look like. I heard him set the date and time for their discussion in Sam's office.

It was a confident call. I could tell that Sam had done most of the talking.

"I guess," Sam said, "we're about to make some changes."

## XXXXI: Changes

*"The only way that we can live, is if we grow. The only way that we can grow is if we change. The only way that we can change is if we learn. The only way we can learn is if we are exposed. And the only way that we can become exposed is if we throw ourselves out into the open. Do it. Throw yourself."* — C. JoyBell C.

A whirlwind of change followed.

16-28: Unleash the Passions of Your Youth…

94

Astonishingly, the situation with Bill simply resolved itself. The prospect of coming in for that face-to-face meeting — the meeting where all the cards would finally be placed on the table — led him to look closely and carefully at his options. He announced his resignation before the meeting even took place. A week later, Sam heard that Bill had checked himself into rehab.

But that wasn't all.

I worked with Sam over the next few months, and the transformation he reported was nothing short of spectacular. Suddenly, he was back in control again — actually, he was in control of his business as he never had been. The whole dynamic of the enterprise changed almost overnight.

Sam was all about business relationships now. He was still proud to run a family-owned business, still happy to make family-friendly decisions for his employees, still eager to support every single one of his people. But the benchmarks had changed. He was no longer trying to protect everyone in the building. He was trying to inspire everyone in the building. And if after a month or so the inspiration didn't take, it was time to move on. And he was hungry to move on now.

A series of remarkable upgrades in the business followed the change in Sam's outlook on his employees — and on his own job. With regular meetings and an evolving strategy through our meetings he rearranged his management team. He started a cross-training initiative that improved efficiency dramatically. He rebranded the business and created a whole new generation of promotional literature. He purchased a new building, and used it to launch a new showroom that won his company all kinds of recognition, visibility, and market share. Soon, he was running

16-28: Unleash the Passions of Your Youth...

95

the largest company of its kind in New England. He had transformed the business.

Six months after our sessions, I got a manila envelope in the mail from him. The letter inside told me that he had grown the business substantially, and thanked me for my help in getting him to where he wanted to go next.

The manila envelope also contained a handwritten essay on Mark Twain's *Huckleberry Finn.* Attached to it was a yellow sticky note that read: "Mrs. Salem: Sorry this was late. Thanks for the extension, and the advice on winning the election."

# The Five Big Lessons to ReIgnite Your Career

As we close, let's look briefly at each of the lessons learned from the five case studies shared in this book. These are the key points, the "big ideas" derived from each main part of the book. It is no exaggeration to say that if you missed even one of these "big ideas," you missed too much. Every one of the key takeaways is important when it comes to making the right decisions for yourself and your company.

On the theory that one can never have too much clarity on a key concept, I'm using this Epilogue to restate, revisit, and reclaim each one of these "big ideas" for you in a concise form. You may wish to come back to this part of the book when you need a quick refresher on the central principles of the 16 - 28 stories I've shared with you here.

## The "Big Idea" Of Part One: The Turning Point Is:

**You have an internal compass, based on one or more key learning experiences from your 16 - 28 years. Once you identify what those compass learning experiences are, you will have a powerful resource for figuring out what does and doesn't match up with who *you* are, both personally and professionally.**

## The "Big Idea" Of Part Two: Bouncing Back Is:

**You have core strengths, aptitudes, and ways of working that began to become clear during your 16-28 years. These are major assets. Before you walk away from a career or business situation that seems to be holding you back, make sure you have identified leveraged those assets to the fullest. You may still be able to create a breakthrough!**

### The "Big Idea" Of Part Three: Freeing Yourself Is:

If you're certain that the 16 - 28 core strengths, aptitudes, and working style you've identified are not supported by your current environment, change that environment. This may mean launching a totally new initiative, such as a startup company or a dramatically different career path.

### The "Big Idea" Of Part Four: Pacing Yourself Is:

You may find yourself in a situation where the full deployment of your 16 - 28 assets is best undertaken in stages. This is particularly likely to be true if you find yourself launching a complex and financially demanding startup venture. Be willing to establish a realistic, workable schedule ... and to move toward your life goal one step at a time.

### The "Big Idea" Of Part Five: Moving On Is:

The clearer you get about the personal, professional, and career objectives of your ideal 16 - 28 self, the more likely it is that you will encounter relationships in your working life that don't support you. Although it may be difficult, you must either improve those relationships so that they *do* support you ... or graduate from them and move on.

I call these the "five big lessons in life and work" because they are, quite literally, the work of a lifetime. Some people go through their entire career without mastering them. With the help of a good Honest Broker, though, you can accelerate the pace at which you make them daily realities of your *working* life. I'd be honored to help you complete that journey. You can always reach me via www.thesuccesscoach.com — and I look forward to the conversation!

16-28: Unleash the Passions of Your Youth...

# Appendix: Notes From My Own 16 - 28 Analysis

It occurred to me that a helpful resource for readers of this book might be a brief overview of what I've learned from my own 16 to 28 period.

As you might imagine, I've spent a fair amount of time analyzing this portion of my life, and the answers I came up with have sometimes been useful in discussions with my clients. There have been a number of times when my own decision to share what I had discovered about myself from examining this critical period of my life helped clients to look more closely at their own 16-28 period, and derive good insights from that period. It's in that spirit of helpfulness that I offer the following observations on the takeaways from my own late adolescence and early adulthood.

In organizing this material, I found that organizing the takeaways by topic, rather than by age, offered a good point of entry for people of all ages.

Please don't imagine that what follows is only of use to someone who is looking back on his or her 16 to 28. It may also be helpful to you if you are currently navigating those early, self-defining years, and looking for the best ways to lay a firm foundation for a happy, fulfilling working life.

## Principle One: Diversity Of Experience.

*"A human being is a part of the whole called by us universe, a part limited in time and space. He experiences himself, his thoughts and feeling as something separated from the rest, a kind of optical delusion of his consciousness. This delusion is a kind of prison for us,*

*restricting us to our personal desires and to affection for a few persons nearest to us. Our task must be to free ourselves from this prison by widening our circle of compassion to embrace all living creatures and the whole of nature in its beauty."* — Albert Einstein

Looking back on the 16 - 28 phase of my life, the main thing I was struck by was that the most significant points of learning and personal development tended to happen whenever I expose myself to new learning environments. This says to me that you, too, should look closely at all of the situations where you were forced out of your comfort zone, given a chance to experience something new and different, and allowed to explore your own natural curiosity about the world This is the time of life when you really want to get out and experiment, try a lot of new things or as I like to say "grow new branches on your tree". So the first and most important principle, if you are looking for lessons from your own 16 to 28, is to look for those times when you tried new ways of living, took on new assignments, joined new clubs, volunteered for new projects, or assumed a learning or leading role of some kind in a discipline that was not familiar to you.

For my part, I was very lucky to have had an extremely diverse set of experiences both before and during college. I went to a top boarding school (Hotchkiss), I studied abroad (Spain), I worked at the State Department (Washington DC) and United Nations (New York), I went to both a large university and a small private college — the list goes on, and I will share more of that list in principles two through five. The big point I want to leave you with here, though, is not that your background needs to look like mine, but that you should look again at your 16 - 28 period if you are of the opinion that "nothing much of interest happened" during this time. This is the typical first response I get when I

16-28: Unleash the Passions of Your Youth…

100

begin to explore these years with clients. It is never true, at least not in my experience in working with people. Inevitably, when I begin pressing the issue, we find that there's at least one experience, and usually between three and five experiences, that were completely new and enriching learning experiences, often quite unexpected at the time: a new job, a summer internship, a vacation trip that led to a new passion or hobby, even a book that had a transformative experience. Look for physical, emotional, and social changes of locale. There are more of them in your personal history than you imagine.

## Principle Two: Leadership Experiences.

*"Leaders are not, as we are often led to think, people who go along with huge crowds following them. Leaders are people who go their own way without caring, or even looking to see, whether anyone is following them. "Leadership qualities" are not the qualities that enable people to attract followers, but those that enable them to do without them. They include, at the very least, courage, endurance, patience, humor, flexibility, resourcefulness, stubbornness, a keen sense of reality, and the ability to keep a cool and clear head, even when things are going badly. True leaders, in short, do not make people into followers, but into other leaders."* — *John Holt*

For most of us, there comes some special opportunity between the years of sixteen and twenty-eight that we decide to seize upon in our emerging adulthood, an opportunity that allows is to take on the role of leadership. This might be on the small scale, in the case of the chance to lead a small extracurricular group of some kind at school; or it might play out on the large scale, as in the choice to start a business. Many entrepreneurs launch their first business venture during the 16-28 window; what matters in

16-28: Unleash the Passions of Your Youth…

101

terms of your emerging identity is not so much whether the business failed or succeeded, but what you learned about yourself as a result of the effort. Whether your leadership experience is large or small in scale, it is always something that allows you to focus on doing something you do well — and permits you to do that center stage. In my case, it was the opportunity to take command of a small group of new acquaintances by working as a tour guide at The Hotchkiss School when I attended at age 16.This experience allowed me to showcase my speaking abilities, connect with people and network, and talk about something I truly loved: the school and the community it served. To prepare for the job, I had to do a significant amount of research and preparation, and to command the attention of the visitors, I had to develop and refine both my people skills and my presentation skills. The job itself was not something I chose to pursue over the long term, but all of those experiences in preparing for the job and learning to do it well were moments of growth and self-awareness. Those moments taught me a lot about myself and what I could accomplish, and they had a major impact on my later professional life. What was your leadership experience?

**Principle Three: Mentorship Experiences.**

*"Hug and kiss whoever helped get you - financially, mentally, morally, emotionally - to this day. Parents, mentors, friends, teachers. If you're too uptight to do that, at least do the old handshake thing, but I recommend a hug and a kiss. Don't let the sun go down without saying thank you to someone, and without admitting to yourself that absolutely no one gets this far alone."* — Stephen King

16-28: Unleash the Passions of Your Youth...

Very often, I find an important component of the sixteen-to-twenty-eight experience is the creation of a critical, transformative relationship with a mentor figure. This mentor figure challenges us, asks us difficult questions, raises our standards, and inspires us to achieve and contribute in ways that might previously have seemed impossible. Not infrequently, the mentor opens doors to new communities, new resources, and new opportunities that carry literally life-changing impact. This relationship with an important early mentor is nearly universal in successful individuals. It is worth examining closely, not only when it emerges, but also in retrospect, because it points us toward key skills, interests, and learning experiences that emerge at the very point of our lives when we are constructing, or refining, our adult identities. In my case, I ended up creating a mentor relationship with Dr. David Larson, my political science professor from college. The relationship opened many new worlds for me, some of which are easy to list here, others of which are harder to map out in words. My mentor convinced me to go for Top Secret clearance so I could apply for an internship at the State Department, which I got. As a result of that experience, working at the State Department, learning a lot about the diplomatic process, and taking part in a research and writing project I would never have undertaken otherwise, and even got wind of a major international incident (Mayaguez – a US ship captured by the Cambodians) three days before *The New York Times* reported it! None of that would have happened if I hadn't had a mentor who was willing to push me, and who expected big things from me.

### Principle Four: Community and Cultural Experiences.

*"Not all those who wander are lost." — J.R.R. Tolkien*

16-28: Unleash the Passions of Your Youth...

103

Here I am referring to experiences that take you, not only out of your comfort zone, but out of your familiar support network. In these types of experiences, you're looking to create brand new relationships in brand new environments that require you to develop brand new languages (literal or figurative). I have already shared a number of these kinds of experiences from my own 16 - 28 period, but this Appendix seems like the right place to share a few more.

When I was 17, I worked as a field hand for a while for a farmer, having gotten to know the local community. I got a sense of life on a 180 acre farm. It was a hard life, picking strawberries and raspberries. This was a kind of physical work I had never done before. That time spent picking fruit helped me to confirm that I had made it past some of the physical limitations that my back injury had left me with (although I only worked 2 - 3 hours at a time), which was a positive experience, but it also gained something much more important: an appreciation of a very different kind of life, a life rooted in respect for the earth and respect for family. This 6 month period I spent on the farm didn't pay much financially, but it did deliver some remarkable returns in terms of my ability to build rapport and establish a common frame of reference with people who might otherwise have seemed so different as to be from another world entirely. The experience means even more to me in retrospect because it connects to a way of life — life on a family farm — that appears to be dying.

Another good area to evaluate carefully in this category is any travel abroad that you've managed to log between the ages of sixteen and twenty-eight. Exposure to different languages, different traditions, and different conceptions of nationality can be transformative learning experiences. That was certainly my experience when I lived with a family in Spain and travelled throughout the country and to neighboring countries.

### Principle Five: "Big Project" Experiences.

*"If a man is called to be a street sweeper, he should sweep streets even as a Michelangelo painted, or Beethoven composed music or Shakespeare wrote poetry. He should sweep streets so well that all the hosts of heaven and earth will pause to say, 'Here lived a great street sweeper who did his job well.'"* — *Martin Luther King, Jr.*

You should also think closely about a Major Project that you undertook and completed to a level of excellence during your 16-28 years.

This should be something you invested significant time, energy, attention, and relationship development capital in. For some people, it's a theatre production; for others, it might be the decision to take on a lead role in the family business; for others, it might be the first big assignment you received after accepting a job offer, the project on which you proved yourself and began building your professional reputation. Whatever it was, it consumed you. It kept you up late at night and got you up early. It gave you your first real personal understanding of what you were capable of, and how high you could set your standards. It challenged you to set your standards even higher next time, and made you redefine yourself, purely in the love of the doing.

For me, the Big Project was a major co-authoring a serious dissertation and textbook on the law of the sea. Co-writing this book and seeing it through the publication process gave me the opportunity to prove myself both as a writer, a researcher, and a creator. It drew ten times out of me than any other project I had committed to up to that point in my life, and gave me a deeper understanding of what was possible when I raised my personal and professional standards to a higher level.

**Principle Six: The "Go For It" Moment.**

*"Remembering that I'll be dead soon is the most important tool I've ever encountered to help me make the big choices in life. Almost everything--all external expectations, all pride, all fear of embarrassment or failure--these things just fall away in the face of death, leaving only what is truly important.... (D)eath is the destination we all share. No one has ever escaped it, and that is how it should be, because death is very likely the single best invention of life. It's life's change agent. It clears out the old to make way for the new."* — Steve Jobs

Most of my clients have identified, at some point in their 16-28 years, a moment at which they decided which passion to focus closely on and committed to doing something that they genuinely loved. For me, that moment was tutoring the kids on that Mohawk Indian reservation in Chicago. This experience of helping others, although it was for only a semester, led to owning a tutoring business, teaching and mentoring at several area universities, working on micro-lending projects in Ecuador and El Salvador with the Quechua Indians, speaking professionally and, of course, executive coaching for business owners and top-performing executives in transition. These all are enriching, empowering and enlightening experiences that allow me to make a difference in the lives of other people, and support them when they are facing unique challenges. The experiences, outlook, and ability that arose from that "Go for It!" moment

16-28: Unleash the Passions of Your Youth…

have allowed me to deliver creative, powerful solutions that have helped clients achieve breakthroughs and gain clarity they need to be more successful in their work, businesses and lives. That experience with the Mohawk Indians has also brought deep and enduring sense of gratitude to my life. It serves as a constant reminder that I owe a debt of sincere thanks to the many mentors, teachers, friends, family and other supporters who reached out and helped me along the way.

## About Doug Campbell III

As an executive and career coach, Doug has worked with thousands of professionals to help them reinvent and achieve new levels of success in their careers, businesses, and working lives. As a professional speaker and member of the National Speakers Association, he has spoken across the country to companies, professional and trade associations, universities, and non-profit organizations.

After his first year at Lake Forest College in Illinois, Doug traveled around the country and photographed nature scenes and people. He sold his color photographs as well as hand-crafted mandalas at Chicago-area art fairs. He also developed a child portrait business from photographic skills learned in high school and from Bob Haiko at the Hotchkiss School in Lakeville, Connecticut.

As a University of New Hampshire undergraduate, Doug worked with Professor David Larson on several independent study projects, and after an internship at the United States Department of State, he co-authored a textbook with Dr. Larson, *Major issues of the Law of the Sea* (University of New Hampshire Press, 1976), which was used at Harvard, Johns Hopkins, and 40 other schools. Doug then consulted for three years on fisheries and marine pollution issues for non-governmental organizations at the United Nations and for the Office of Technology Assessment of the US Congress.

Since he had studied abroad and written on his travels in Spain for the college newspaper, his next venture was to launch a weekly newspaper (as a minority partner) with an experienced newspaper professional, Davis Kennedy, and a well-known

16-28: Unleash the Passions of Your Youth...

publisher, Jim Coldsmith. *The Port Packet* grew rapidly, and became the most widely circulated paper in Alexandria, Virginia.

After completing his MBA at the Darden School at the University of Virginia, Doug worked in strategic planning and as a product manager with Mike Corey before becoming Chief Marketing Officer for Champion Office products (COP), a $200 million division of Champion International with 23 locations in Stamford, Connecticut. He worked extensively with Xerox, IBM, Pitney Bowes, and also managed the COMDEX tradeshow for COP, in Las Vegas and Atlanta.

In 1985, Doug opened the first Sylvan Learning Center K-12 tutoring franchise on the East Coast. The facility was located in Darien, Connecticut, and was launched with his wife Gwynne. Top local educators were helpful and supportive of the new business. He also helped launch Sylvan's national advertising campaign, and served as vice chairman of the Franchise Owners' Association with its chairman, Dick McSorley. (Doug had worked to establish that organization, which represented owners' interests at Sylvan.)

In 1987, Doug taught management, marketing, human resources, strategy and entrepreneurship courses to undergraduate and MBA students at Fairfield University and Sacred Heart University in Connecticut. He also cofounded *Vanguard: the Connecticut Journal of Business and Entrepreneurship* with Dr. Lawrence Weinstein.

In 1996, Doug spoke at the International Coaching Federation's annual conference in Houston, and his business The Success Coach was launched. He worked with executive coaches Charlie Miller and John Tessier in his early years as an executive coach. Clients have included Cort Furniture Rentals, Exposures, Boardroom Reports, Sobe, boattest.com, Spinnaker Real Estate
16-28: Unleash the Passions of Your Youth...

Partners, Trammel Crow, Cable Ready, Win Wholesale, and many others.

Doug has been profiled in *The Wall Street Journal*, *Bottom Line Business*, the *Stamford Advocate*, and *Investors Business Daily*. He is also a business insights expert for Wells Fargo Bank. He has been interviewed on Cablevision and WOR radio, and is a member of the brain trust for Jim Blasingame's small business radio network. In 2009 he published his book, *Where to Go From Here: Reinventing Your Career, Your Business, Your Working Life*.

Doug coaches one-on-one and also conducts workshops on Leadership & Team Building, Networking Strategies That Really Work, and Business Strategy for "key" managers with companies, trade associations and non-profits. He is active in the International Coaching Federation (he ran workshops at the national conference), National Speakers Association, American Marketing Association, the Connecticut Venture Group, The American Society of Training & Development, Toastmasters, the Dutch Treat Club, and numerous chambers and business organizations.

Doug's extensive and varied experiences with all forms of business have contributed to his understanding of clients' issues and his work with them. Doug lives in Darien Connecticut, with his wife. He is actively involved with a Darien-based nonprofit that works closely with WorldVision and provides consulting and gift capital to microfinance institutions in El Salvador, Ecuador, the Dominican Republic, and Senegal.

16-28: Unleash the Passions of Your Youth...

# My 16 – 28 passions Worksheet
## Here Are Some Activities in My Current Life That Come From My 16 - 28 Passions

| 16 - 28 passions | Activities now |
|---|---|
| Majored in Spanish & International Relations | Microlending Ecuador & El Salvador (1999-present) |
| Worked at United Nations; US Department of State | Microlending |
| Co-Author *Major Issues of the Law of the Sea* | Author *Where To Go From Here: Reinventing Your Career and Your Business* **(2009)** |
| Tutor American Indian kids in Chicago | Co-Owner Sylvan Learning Center (1984-present) |
| Started Alexandria Packet – weekly newspaper | Columnist for CT & NY weeklies (1998-present) |
| Started Entrepreneurs Club at Darden UVA | Coach CEOs, Executives, Business Owners (1996-present) |
| College Golf Coach | Wilton CT High School Golf Coach (2005-2009) |
| Child Portrait Photography business | |

| 16-28 Passions | Activities Now |
|----------------|----------------|
|                |                |
|                |                |
|                |                |
|                |                |
|                |                |
|                |                |
|                |                |

16-28: Unleash the Passions of Your Youth…

16-28: Unleash the Passions of Your Youth…

16-28: Unleash the Passions of Your Youth…

www.ingramcontent.com/pod-product-compliance
Lightning Source LLC
Chambersburg PA
CBHW071200200326
41519CB00018B/5295